Praise for

"The prognosis for the aging baby-boomer business owner in today's market is one of a healthy and happy retirement, provided time-sensitive attention to detail is maintained. There is no doubt the benefits of effective planning and a fundamental understanding of the nuances of selling a business are innate across all industries and market sectors. The Exit Equation addresses these issues head-on. David has again provided business owners the insight and perspective needed to make informed decisions on a very important topic."

- **Mark T. Murphy, DDS, FAGD**

Vice President of Clinical Education for DTI Dental Technologies Inc.-Microdental. Dr. Murphy also serves as Lead Faculty for Mercer Advisors, Adjunct Faculty for the University of Michigan Dental School and Visiting Faculty at the Pankey Institute. He serves on the IdentAlloy Council, the Foundation Board for the National Association of Dental Labs and on The Pankey Institute Board of Directors. Dr. Murphy is a noted speaker on dental practice operations.

~ ~ ~ ~ ~ ~

"Entrepreneurs are unique individuals who possess strong drive, unusual persistence, and the uncanny ability to make something out of nothing more than a simple vision. What really sets them apart is that they actually do it, rather than just talking about it. They tend to be really good at starting things and growing it once it's started, but they often fall short when it comes to exiting well, or even exiting gracefully. Because of the entrepreneur's singular focus on starting, growing and nurturing his dream, when it comes to successful exit strategies for the business he can fall tragically short of the mark. David has provided crucial insights and concrete steps necessary for every entrepreneur who wants to transition himself from successful business owner to successful retired business owner. The Exit Equation is witty, pointed and a good kick-in-the-pants."

- **Bob Stefanski Esq.**

Bob is a technology entrepreneur and investor based in Palo Alto, CA. He was on the founding management team of TIBCO Software, the leading pure play enterprise infrastructure software company in the world, and actively advises start-up companies in the software, mobile and Internet markets. He previously practiced law in New York City at the international law firm of Weil, Gotshal & Manges, where he represented software companies and sports and entertainment organizations, including the NBA Players Association and the NFL Players Association.

THE EXIT EQUATION

How to Leave Your Business with Your Money and On Your Terms

Tars —
Thank you for all you have done over the years. I hope you enjoy the book since you lived it not too long ago.

David Saint-Onge

Copyright © 2012 by David Saint-Onge

ISBN-13: 978-0-9834510-1-3

All rights reserved.

No part of this publication may be reproduced, stored in a retrieval system or transmitted in any form or by any means electronic, mechanical, photocopying, recording or otherwise, without the prior written permission of the author or publisher (except in the case of a reviewer, who may quote brief passages in a review).

Legal Disclaimer

The Publisher and the Author make no representations or warranties with respect to the accuracy or completeness of the contents of this work and specifically disclaim all warranties, including without limitation warranties of fitness for a particular purpose. No warranty may be created or extended by sales or promotional materials. The advice and strategies contained herein may not be suitable for every situation.

Neither the Publisher nor the Author shall be liable for damages arising herefrom. The fact that an organization or website is referred to in this work as a citation and/or a potential source of further information does not mean the Author or the Publisher endorses the information the organization or website may provide or recommendations it may make.

Further, readers should be aware that internet websites listed in this work may have changed or ceased since this work was written.

Acknowledgements

I want to walk the same roads as everybody else, through the trees and past the gates, getting high on heavenly breezes and making new friends along the way.

I won't ask much of nobody.

I am just here to sing along, and make my mistakes look gracious and learn some lessons from my wrongs.

- Sunshine Song, Jason Mraz

It is interesting how life evolves. There is no way of knowing what awaits us as we approach each fork in the road of our professional path. In the end, we are responsible to ourselves; everything else takes care of itself if we take care of ourselves.

I am privileged to have had the opportunity to make mistakes, and honored to have learned from them. I sincerely appreciate the love of my wife Kris, and children Collin and Carley, as well as my family and friends. I am forever indebted to their support and patience. I can be a difficult person to understand and tolerate. But at the end of the day, I don't view the glass as either half full or half empty; I believe the glass should be full all the time. Yes, it can be construed as a defeatist attitude, but it has carried me through the times I questioned my own ability.

Many thanks to all who have supported me. You have blessed me more than I deserve and I will never forget your loyalty.

Contents

Prologue: Getting Out Now, Getting Out Happy 11

Chapter 1: Lifetime Rewards: The Business Sales Indicator 25
    The Seven Step "Rewards" Plan to Letting Go and Winning Big 27
    Step 1: Reviewing & Balancing Your Checkbook 29
    Step 2: Evaluating & Differentiating Needs From Wants 33
    Step 3: Weighing the Pros and Cons 35
    Step 4: Accepting the Truth 37
    Step 5: Revising Your Short-Term Business Strategy 39
    Step 6: Deciding on a Plan of Action 41
    Step 7: Selling Your Business: The Time Value of Money Time vs. Rewards 42

Chapter 2: The Basis of the Exit Plan 45
    Your Economic Countdown 48
    Why an Exit Strategy? 51
    Succession Depression: Handing Over the Reigns 56
    Shooting From the Hip Does Not Work 58
    The Emotional Tug of War 62
    Averting Your Greatest Regret 64

Chapter 3: Plan Your Work and Work Your Plan 69
    With Planning, Good Things Happen 72
    Create a Timetable to Leave Your Company – 3 to 5 Years 75
    Taking the Baby Steps 78
    Understanding Your Company 86
    How Do You Make Money? 89

    Mirror on the Wall 90
    Building the Yellow Brick Road 92
    Don't Cook the Books 93
    Stick to the Script — the Most Difficult Thing an Owner Must Do 95

Chapter 4: The Three Most Important Things in Business & in Departing Your Company 97
    Cash Flow, Cash Flow, Cash Flow 101
    Operating Cash Flow 103
    Investment Cash Flow (aka Free Cash Flow) 104
    Financing Cash Flow 105
    Create Your Own Buy-Out Scenario 106
    Management Buy-Out 107
    Selling to Family 109
    Selling to Another Company 112
    Self-Financing the Sale 113
    Liquidation 115
    Sell With the Right Attitude 115

Chapter 5: The Cost of Doing Business and Impact on the Deal . 119
    Knowing Your Company 123
    Understanding Your Competitive Advantage 125
    Where Do You Spend Your Money? 127
    Protecting Your Sacred Cows 129
    Sacrificial Lambs 130
    Where Have You "Missed"? 133
    Are You the Industry Leader or a Follower? 134

Chapter 6: Systems Work When You Don't 137
    Would Your Company Benefit From Systems? 142
    Document, Document, Document 145
    How to Create Efficiency 147
    How Systems Sell Your Business 150

Chapter 7: Forget Chapter 6: What Really Sells a Company? 153
Start With the Easy One: Terms 157
General Advice About Negotiating Terms 164
Now, the Hard One: Cash 165

Chapter 8: Willing Buyers & Willing Sellers: Follow the Yellow Brick Road 171
Willing Buyers, Willing Sellers and Fair Market Value 174
Price Versus Value 175
How to Value Your Company 176
Forget a Magic Formula 178
Are You Pricing Your Company Out of the Market? 179
Deal-Making 182

Chapter 9: The Art of the Exit: Get What You Need—and It's Not Always Dollars 187
The Pendulum Swings 191
Ask Yourself the Tough Questions 194
Procrastination Is the Enemy 196

Chapter 10: An Internal Sale: The Golden Rules 201
Option 1: Family Succession 205
Fair Doesn't Necessarily Mean Equal 208
Remember, It's Business Not Family 210
Option 2: Management Team Succession 211
Option 3: Selling to a Key Employee 215
The View From the Big Chair 217
Accept Your New Role 220

Chapter 11: An External Sale 223
Come Out, Come Out Wherever You Are 226
Acquisition in Detail 227
Selling to a Competitor 229
Important Reminders Are Worth Repeating 231

Chapter 12: An Absentee Owner: Staying in the Game 235
    Could You Be an Absentee Owner?...238
    Transitioning Into an Absentee Owner 244
    Monitoring Your Company 244
    Letting Go of the Control Freak Within You...245
    Keeping Relationships 246

Chapter 13: The Underlying Principles of *The Exit Equation*......... 249

Chapter 14: Epilogue 263

Prologue:
Getting Out Now,
Getting Out Happy

"The victorious strategist only seeks battle after the victory has been won, whereas he who is destined to defeat, first fights and afterwards looks for victory." — **Sun Tzu**

Everyone dreams of fairytale endings. You did, which is why you started a business all those years ago. You dreamed of respect, of money — and the intoxicating freedom that comes from being your own boss. We all know money and freedom are interdependent; it is impossible to have one without the other. Every action, every wish, every dream in your life has been based on the amount of money you've been able to earn. Who you are, and what you have achieved, has inevitably been rooted in your financial situation.

But the world is not a fairytale; and things don't necessarily go as planned. You have worked very hard and you are starting to wonder whether you will ever be able to reach that elusive "retirement", you have dreamed of in recent years. That's what your business was to you in those early days — a ticket to cash and the freedom that comes with it.

You had a plan once, do you remember? Start a business, work hard while you can, and retire a wealthy person. Then, perhaps, see the world, invest in new business opportunities, buy that seaside or golf condo you've always wanted and have enough to live comfortably for the rest of your life.

At the outset of this Prologue, there is a quote from Sun Tzu's *Art of War* that defines the leading problem for thousands of business owners all across America. You've done a great job with your business, but how do you get out? Can your business survive without you? Should you sell it, and if so, when and how? How do you get out and *be happy?*

Like many of your peers, you charged into business without an exit strategy. You have worked for decades without really considering what you are going to do when it's time to quit. This book will enlighten you on the Exit Equation, how to walk and not run toward a plan that is well-thought out, effective, and gives you the peace of mind that you did it right, for the right reasons, under the right expectations, and for the right price. By the end, you will not only know what you need to do and how to do it, but you will be able to live without regret.

Is Now the End of Your Career?

Time is money, and money is freedom. One of the biggest problems with owning and running your business is that you have not been able to bridge the time/money divide. How could you, with employees to look after , financial records to keep, and customers to find?

Imagine how much time you would have if you no longer had to run your business! Better yet, how much money would you have if you sold your business for what it's worth? To finally bridge this cavernous divide that has kept you from freedom and enjoying your life, you need to better understand the nuances of the exit.

Are you ready to sell your business and walk away? There are so many reasons why you could say no. Perhaps you have cash flow concerns; or maybe you are too intertwined in the daily performance of your company. Maybe you have burdened yourself with a shared equity relationship with some of your key employees, and you are not sure how this relationship will be addressed if you were to leave first. Whatever your situation, you need to cut through the layers of guilt, obligation, and that deep-seated sense of responsibility you feel and come to an honest reality. *How and when do I exit my company?*

Out of Control, To Gain Control

Conceptually, it is easy to sell your business. Functionally, it is another thing to sell it and finally be relieved of the constant pressure and stress and the endlessly long days of hard work. This does not always happen, as many business owners are trapped in their businesses and either don't or won't find a way out that makes sense. The thing is, you deserve the rewards of a lifetime's worth of work. If you take the time to fully understand how an effective exit strategy should be conceived, designed, and implemented, you will finally realize your fears are overblown and your ability to live constructively and productively outside of your company can be achieved. You are not alone.

After all, you built your business from nothing. It is yours and as much a part of your life as your family and friends. How could you let it go? Let us go out on a limb and reaffirm some not so nice, but very relevant, truths about the world.

Money equates to freedom. The more money you have, the happier you are. But it is not money we crave—it is the experiences that come from it. This is especially true with entrepreneurs and small business owners. You understand that money is a means to an end. Out of all the currencies on earth, the American dollar has always been synonymous with finding the freedom that leads to happiness. It is programmed into us from a young age.

We idolize people who have a lot of money and call them "extraordinary," or "celebrity"; and all because they have what we want—a way to be happy. Our collective goal as business owners is to cast off the chains of debt and hard work and live unburdened by those who want something from us. All of us desperately want this goal to become a reality, and it becomes of greater importance as we get older.

Success and happiness in life is a function of freedom to do what you want, when you want. Too many business owners tend to focus on false ambitions—thinking that their time and money is better served through the success of their businesses. This is the real reason why business owners reject the chance to be happy when they come to the end of their careers. The plan was always work, get rich, have fun. Somewhere between working, earning, and living—the end goal is forgotten. Life happens; bills happen; and wealth and freedom never seem to come.

Now you find yourself approaching the end of your career. You once again have the opportunity to reap the rewards of your hard work and risk-taking. Only you cannot; or for too many business owners, you will not. For some of you, the light at the end of the tunnel has gone out. All you can do now is hope to keep things going. Stay in control. Work. This is not good for you, and it may not be good for your business either. Letting go of your business is going to be a battle. It will affect you emotionally, spiritually, physically, and financially.

In the next five to ten years, Baby Boomers in the U.S. will have to sell or refinance their companies—over 12,000,000 of them—in order to retire. You have a choice. Learn how to prepare for your own happy ending, or allow your business to consume what time, money, and happiness you have left.

Believe it or not, you have a number of options. This book is going to help you figure out exactly which of these will benefit you the most. Retirement from a business that you have owned can come in many forms. You can sell it to your employees or a competitor or maybe even give it to your children. You may even choose to go into liquidation. It seems simple, but it is the most weighty and crucial decision of your career and probably the one deal you have never done before.

One wrong move and you will never experience the satisfaction of a work career well spent.

Duty or Retreat? Try Duty to Retreat

Selling your business will be complicated. You will overvalue it because of the time you have spent making it work. All deals have strings attached to them. You could end up selling your business and then be forced to operate it until the day you die. If you give it to your children, will your involvement really be over? If you sell it for less than it's worth, will you have to find another job to fully realize your retirement dream? These are just some of the bridges you might have to cross as you become serious about the notion of leaving.

However, these can all be sorted out with an exit strategy that takes into account why you want to leave; when you want to leave; how you will leave; how much money your business is really worth; and what you will do when you are gone. You have to develop a plan of attack that puts you first. This stage of your career is a battle. Whether it's pride, responsibility, or duty that keeps you from making the right decisions, you have to find your way back to what matters. If you are seeing this opportunity as duty or retreat, or if this decision centers more on your responsibility not to let everyone down, such thinking is not going to help you.

In law, duty to retreat has a significant meaning. It is used in cases where self-defense is called into question. In other words, the accused must prove they had no choice but to defend themselves from harm. Specifically, this term is used to describe someone that has actively sought to avoid conflict before having to use defensive tactics. This is not unlike the battle between you and your business.

Many business owners decide to continue working, and they let their circumstances destroy their chances of ever being happy. They choose duty over retreat because their mindset is never challenged. When you reconnect with your goals in life and begin planning an exit strategy, you change duty or retreat into *duty to retreat*. It becomes your goal once again—to fight against the traps in life that keep you down.

You should not have to deal with this at the end of your career. Yet too many highly educated and high performing people do. They choose to resign themselves to an unfortunate fate—working well into their retirement years—instead of embracing the chance to be happy. As we spoke about earlier, happiness at its core centers on money and freedom. If your business provides the money you need but it also demands your freedom, is there any chance for you to be happy? These are the new ideals that will help you leave your working life behind.

This is the one point in your career when you cannot afford to give in. You have a duty to yourself to understand what makes you happy and to engage in a strategy where you can now begin to enjoy the fruits of your hard work. Retirement is supposed to be a renewal of your love for life and exploration. To accomplish this goal, it is imperative that your business be sold wisely and shrewdly.

Do not let your own mind trick you into thinking that a running business means you are successful or dutiful. Over the course of your professional career, you have accumulated quite a personal tab—and now's the time to get it paid back in full.

Why So Many Business Owners Lose Out

As you get older, you start thinking less about your own happiness and more about the happiness of the people you care about. It is human nature to want to see your family thrive and prosper.

Unfortunately, it is this train of thought that ends up derailing your life. When you approach retirement age, you come to the realization that things change. The resounding societal chorus tells you that you are somehow less important than you used to be; that you are meant to step aside and let the younger generation have their time.

The reality is that the baby boomer generation lost a lot, thanks to shifting economies, war, and recession. Many people just like you cannot really survive on their pensions. With prices skyrocketing and inflation looming with every year that goes by, your retirement income continues to depreciate. Is this the reward you want or deserve after working your entire life? Enough is enough. In many ways it boils down to the notion of retire or die.

So why do so many business owners lose out on their opportunity to embrace a wealthy, happy retirement? There are several reasons, many of which you are probably currently experiencing. If your business has been your world for decades, its sentimental value could be holding you back. Your attachment to your company may prevent you from ever letting go, or even considering a business sale.

The reason you started your business was to make money. The reason many never make money is because they become emotionally entangled with their businesses. Getting by is not living, just like buying cheap groceries isn't eating or going away for the weekend every now and then isn't traveling. When did retirement become about resignation and depression? Why do you think that you have to lose out at all?

Learning about the art of an effective and promising exit strategy is more than just a plan; it is preparation with culmination. The process of leaving your company the right way takes preparation. The culmination of these efforts is coming to peace with yourself in the process and choosing the right road to take at the end of your career. Whether you aim to leave your business to a family member or sell it to a stranger, you are the one who is at risk. The real reason why business owners lose out is that they don't view the end of their business careers as a risk. Truth be told, leaving your business will actually make or break your career. Forget the thousands of reasons why you should not sell and complete your life's mission! If it takes you five years of strategic planning and implementation, at least you have an end goal. Selling your business to retire is not the end of your life. You may feel it is because you will lose that sense of purpose, that reason to keep going.

As you prepare to leave your business, you are going to have to deal with a rollercoaster of emotions. Don't let those around you fool you into making the wrong decisions for the wrong reasons. The forces at work in your life shouldn't make you deviate from the end result. Money, freedom, and happiness are available to you, if you only learn how to invite them in. It is time to put your interests ahead of everyone else. Keep the prize in sight, so you do not lose out.

The Implications of DIY Ownership

Your business is an extension of who you are. You have had a hand in every little detail, from the startup phase to now. Have you spent time delegating; teaching other employees how to handle the things you've been doing for years? Being a strong leader means being a good teacher. This single statement could shatter your dreams of retirement. Many owners have never taken the time to effectively delegate critical aspects of business operations to their staff. They have held fast to the belief that ownership is a do-it-yourself (DIY) task.

If you are fast approaching retirement age—or have already arrived—this is one problem you need to sort out. This might be the most dangerous form of ownership because it prevents you from ever having the option to retire. If you feel that without you, your business would fail, it's time to change the way you run it. This risk factor must not be ignored. It ties you into every deal you might make with a buyer and could significantly limit the value of your business.

The notion that your business relies on your input as a critical variable to the business' success is a contagion to your departure. It devalues the business and prevents you from leaving your company with your money. In an ideal situation, you want to be able to leave your business forever as it continues to churn sales and profits like an efficient machine.

In many ways and across many types of businesses, buyers know that a business is only as good as its employees. If you have taken the time to instill that same passion, knowledge, and desire for success in your employees, then your business is more likely to sell for a great price. Being the primary strategist, manager, business developer and key employee may be a wonderful ego stroke for you, but it does little to attract a premium buyer for your business.

Being "the man," working all the time, and not being in a position to be your own person has a diminishing attraction. This is only worsened when your personal money and the business' money is indistinguishable. Recognizing these pitfalls and how they become the impetus for the stress you live with every day is important. As you age, you cannot carry these burdens without experiencing their harmful effects on your health. In a way, this is no different than being addicted to alcohol, cigarettes, or prescription drugs. Being trapped in a business you come to despise is but one of the implications of DIY ownership you need to recognize and commit to changing. It's so important, it's in the Prologue to this book. Sun Tzu knew that when faced with an imminent battle, the best hope for victory was to put his trust in the people around him; not because he had no choice, but because he'd instilled his own lessons in them and fully understood their capabilities.

If you are a DIY owner, implementation of your retirement exit strategy may take longer than other business owners who have fixed this flaw. But don't fret; it doesn't mean you have to give up on the expectation of freedom and happiness. It just means that you have a bit more work to do before you can enjoy the benefits of your departure. Let's be honest—you're no stranger to hard work! Today is the first day of your ownership makeover. Inside these pages, you will learn what it means to take responsibility for the outcome of your actions.

The Business 360 and Your Money Concerns

It is a strange feeling—preparing for the end of what has been your entire working life. But the science of business is as much about starting as it is about ending.

Once you come to the realization as to why you want to leave your business and what will be important to you when you do decide to leave, the next center of your attention turns to cash. How much is your business really worth? Who are you going to sell it to? How can you get the most money out this deal? Will you get your money paid in a lump sum or over time? Will you have to finance the note, or will you have to stay on and perform to ensure you ultimately get your money? It's called the Business 360, and it is all about the money.

To orientate yourself in your future sale, you will have to do some calculations. Nothing serious, but this is something that will make all the difference. If you had to retire tomorrow, how much money would you need? What is worth noting is that real wealth is not made simply by starting a company; and it's not made simply by growing your company. Real wealth is made by selling your company, and particularly, selling to an acquirer who will pay a premium because it believes it can generate even more value from what you've built.

Try seeing your business through the eyes of a buyer. What's wrong with it? Where can it be improved? A common problem with owning a business for a long time is that things get stagnant. It's not unheard of for business owners to wait too long to sell and end up with an undervalued product.

The Exit Equation is going to take you through your paces. You will discover why, how, and when to leave your company and formulate a strategy that will lead you to financial freedom.

Your mindset will change as you begin to accept and implement tactics in business that will eventually improve your life. You don't have to second-guess yourself or spend the rest of your life living with regret. This book is about embracing the final stage in your career. It is about surpassing your own expectations for your future. Certainly, it discusses the money aspect of your departure—but it is also about rediscovering the happiness you have been working towards for years.

Finally, you will become a strategic player, mastering your business when it matters most. *The Exit Equation* was written for every small business owner out there, so they can achieve the ultimate sale and the joy that comes from a plan well played.

> *This may come as a complete surprise to you, but there is nothing wrong with expecting a fairytale ending.*

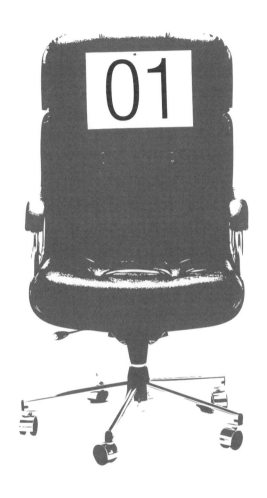

Lifetime Rewards:
The Business Sales Indicator

The Seven Step "Rewards" Plan to Letting Go and Winning Big

Some time ago, I was enjoying a few drinks around the campfire with a couple of friends. As was typically the case, the conversation fell on our businesses and the challenges we routinely faced. Each person had concerns, and we spoke frankly about our ideal retirement plans. One by one, everyone described what they wanted for the future. I was surprised at how different each of the opinions was about the "perfect" retirement scenario.

One friend did not even consider the fact that he would never work again. All he wanted to do was work from home — as long as his home was on a beach. The others explained how they would prefer to travel, settle in a warmer climate, or invest some cash in something new that would help supplement their monthly income. None of them were really sure how they would achieve these goals.

On the drive home, I started asking myself some tough questions. If I were in a position to sell my company now, would I do it? There was a distinctly anxious feeling in the pit of my stomach. I am not much different from any other small business owner, and my views of my business ownership and the notion of selling are not much different from how a lot of people feel about their businesses. I came to the simple reality that a business owner spends so much time and effort at work that walking away would feel like a betrayal. I felt that even if I did sell, I would not be happy about it. And even worse than that, I had no idea what I'd do once my business was sold.

As I contemplated this issue, I kept coming back to the same reality: business owners are cut from the same cloth. Our business gives our life purpose. So many business owners are go-getters, self-starters, and born to be in control. These are purpose-driven lives. From a young age, you realize that you have leadership ability, new ideas, and the potential to make great things happen for yourself. To lose this sense of purpose is perhaps the most difficult adjustment you will ever make.

When reflecting on that campfire discussion, I came away with the understanding that a person's emotions often get in the way of making the right decisions. As business owners, we've poured our heart and soul into our business; we have made critical decisions before, so why should the ideal of being happy be any different? At some point before retirement, we will have to learn to let go. This could result in a happier life or a deep-seated sense of loss that never goes away. Everyone wants to feel useful—that they're worth something to the people in their lives. Selling our business tends to throw a cog in our well-oiled life's work machine.

Because you and I are no different than other small business owners, you are probably asking yourself, "Sure, I'd love to retire and enjoy my money and my time, but it's not that easy; how do I even begin the process?" The process of self-evaluation begins with a series of important steps you need to walk yourself through before you can claim all of the well-earned rewards of your life's work. These steps will help clarify your real opinion on retirement and what you're heading towards. You will then be able to adjust your behavior and work towards the retirement you actually desire. It is only through this process that, when you do decide to sell your business or pass the torch, your life will once again be filled with purpose.

It is up to you to find that new purpose inside yourself and push towards it with all your might. Whether you like it or not, you're likely finding yourself in a position to start making plans for the twilight years that lay ahead. If you do it right, good things happen. If you wait and are forced to make hasty decisions, you will likely become dissatisfied and filled with regret.

Step 1: Reviewing & Balancing Your Checkbook

Take a step back for a moment. Do you have a business exit strategy, or do you just plan to address this issue when the time comes? Remember how you went about planning your business before you started it? Taking the time to understand the market and your competitors; figuring out where to locate your business and what you needed to get off the ground; talking to business associates, confidants, and family about what you wanted to do and how you wanted to do it; making sure you thought of all the important things so you didn't waste your time and money?

Nearing the end of your business life requires just as much work—only now, you have to deal with the surrounding complications that have influenced every facet of your life. Be honest—the process of leaving your company is just as important as starting your company.

Your work has been a dominant force in your life, and now, as you contemplate how to exit it, you are beginning to realize your life has become unbalanced. If you continue on this path, you may never retire. You might end up losing your business anyway or giving it away—because you just don't have the energy to deal with daily stresses anymore.

This is your wake up call.

If you are reading this book, you are likely closing in on retirement age and you have no real exit strategy in play. There are a lot of reasons why this has happened, some of which you may not want to admit. Does being a business owner make you proud? Do you feel good about working for yourself? Does the inherent risk-taking of being your own boss get the competitive juices flowing? Chances are, if you sit back for just a minute and contemplate your average day and the issues you need to address as part of the responsibility of owning your own business, you will come to the conclusion that it is time to *balance your checkbook*—not only in the financial sense, but in every other possible sense that makes up your life.

Each day you wake up. You get dressed and go to work. You deal with customers, staff, complaints, issues, money, and future plans. If you are not at work doing these things, I bet you are doing them at your kid's ball game or while you are sitting with your significant other at dinner, or while you are driving down the road. In reality, you are not working to live, you are living to work. This is a habit you need to break if you want to eventually leave your business on your terms and with your money.

As you stand right now, maybe you cannot afford to exit your company. Maybe the economy has caused your cash reserves to dwindle, or you have had to reinvest additional equity into your company. Perhaps your business operations are not conducted in a truly efficient manner and your profitability suffers. This issue could prevent you from getting all your equity out of the business if you tried to sell it now. Yes, there are many issues that may prevent you from exiting now, but these are all fixable.

It may not even be about money. Are there just too many things you do for your business that keep it going? Maybe you are the primary business development person for your company, and everyone wants to deal with you. Perhaps you have not instilled the right training and quality assurance processes into your company, and you find yourself always fixing the little things that make a huge difference. These are just some of the realities of being your own boss, and these issues prevent you from achieving escape velocity.

In the end, it is about balancing your checkbook; coming to a conclusion that the means has an end and that the end is something you need and want. But if you are like many business owners, your personal checkbook (e.g., family, social, religious, and civic) is not balanced. Your commitment to your business overrides your commitment to your life.

When this happens, you begin to realize the path you are on will not support your departure from your company. You have become so intertwined with your company, you couldn't leave even if you wanted to. Your vacation schedule, personal finances, social events, club memberships, and even the personal vehicle you drive are somehow determined by your company and its needs. This is a suction that can be difficult to acknowledge, let alone break. The path to successfully exiting your company starts with taking stock of where your life is and where it's heading.

For many business owners, having an unbalanced checkbook is not uncommon. You have had to apportion a large amount of your time to work. You have built relationships around your corporate identity. Your needs have been based around work, and your life has conformed to this goal. But in the next few years, these needs will change. Work will fall away, and what will you have left?

The first step of your exit strategy is to see where your life is heading right now. Strip away the opinions and excuses, and acknowledge that it is time for a change. If you leave it, or put it off, or make the wrong decisions in the end—how will you ever be happy? How will you ever be able to enjoy the happiness that comes from a fulfilled life of rewards?

Every objective has a task; every task has a metric; every metric can be quantified and assessed as a success or a failure. If your objective is to depart your company on your terms with your money, there are a series of tasks to be strategized and achieved. In the end, the true measure of your accomplishments and worth as a business owner relies solely on your happiness when you walk out the office door for the last time. Nothing else matters, and nothing is more important, because in the end, they will forget your name; they will forget your attention to detail; and they will forget all the good you accomplished. In the end, you have to realize that your life goes on as well.

Find out where you are heading now so that you can get on with the business of living.

Step 2: Evaluating & Differentiating Needs From Wants

As you get older, your physical, emotional, and spiritual needs are amplified. Everyone has dreams of what their retirement is going to be like. Usually, it includes new places, relaxation, and enjoying the things you have missed during your work life. It sounds like paradise — or does it? The years, months, days, and hours of your life will still roll by. The only difference is that they will not be consumed by work.

How often will you travel, buy something you've always wanted, or simply become reacquainted with old friends? How will you value your free time? Will your average post-retirement day be challenging enough? These questions are terrifying to many business owners who face retirement. The days lose their meaning. Your fast-paced life comes to a grinding, almost unpleasant halt. And all too often, retirees simply don't have the money to continue living the lifestyle they want and expect.

Once the sale of your business is completed, and you finally realize the permanence of the decision — will you be able to fill your life with the things that make you happy? Will you find purpose again? Similar to the start-up phase of your company or a significant growth phase you may have navigated, new experiences contribute to a happy life. In many ways, the process of starting and growing your business is no different than starting and growing your life after you have stepped away from your business. Step 2 of your exit strategy is about evaluating and differentiating your needs from your wants.

Whether your daily life as a business owner was predicated on staying physically fit, being true to your purpose and moral ideals, or using your wealth and influence to serve a greater good, your retirement years can, and should, serve similar purposes. But what must be understood by a business owner who is about to liquidate his or her equity is that purpose must still be defined. It is vitally important to strategize and plan your post-ownership years with the same passion and purpose you did when you started, purchased, and grew your business. It is what you do, so why stop now?

There may even come a time as you start to plan for your post-ownership years that perhaps you may even want to improve your lifestyle! Give more of yourself to the people you love, or spend more time doing what matters most to you. Because when you depart your business, there will be a void you need to fill. Will you be prepared for the inevitability of reinventing yourself? The greater your affinity with your business (the dominant force i1n your life up to this point) the more your judgment is clouded. When balancing needs and wants, you must extract your current beliefs from the demands of your business.

Time without freedom can be a terrible burden. As the baby boomer generation moves toward retirement, the truth is that many former business owners will not be able to maintain their old lifestyles. A diminishing economy and bad planning will sure make this premonition a reality. These last few years before you exit your company will dictate the quality of the remainder of your life.

The realities you faced when you were 30 years of age either gave you the courage to do what you wanted or forced you to take a risk. In either case, you made your decisions and blazed the trail. No doubt, you had responsibilities to your family, friends, and colleagues. You realized that working hard early meant a secure, happy life at the end. And just like that, time blew by in a haze of hard work, time commitments, and payroll deadlines. Now you find yourself contemplating an exit from your company.

I trust you understand the concept of a bucket list. Many people wrongfully think a bucket list is some kind of repentance for things not done in life. But truth be told, a bucket list is the plans, aspirations, and achievements to live for. These are the "wants" in your life, not simply the "needs."

Make a list of the most important things in your life. Think hard about what you're going to do with your retirement. Are they probable and possible? Once you begin to see yourself as a whole and begin to separate your personal identity from your business, you will start to achieve escape velocity. Your happiness and fulfillment comes from wanting to achieve it, not from merely needing to do it.

Step 3: Weighing the Pros and Cons

There are pros and cons to every decision and every action. As a business owner, you understand the obviousness of the statement, and you have inevitably picked the right direction to turn more times than not when you come to a fork in the road. In each instance, you completed your due diligence, made your decision, and then blazed forward. The same is true when faced with life-altering decisions. No one can tell you what to do; you have to figure that out for yourself. The same can be said about exiting your business. Step 3 in the process of developing an effective exit strategy is about acknowledging the fork in the road and giving your due diligence to make a decision you will ultimately have to live with.

Sell now or stay on a little while longer? If you are mentally ready to retire, you will need to address whether you are physically ready. Rushing into it may result in selling your business for less than what it's worth and ruining a secure financial future. Selling without an effective strategy in place will, almost assuredly, result in critical mistakes. Pushing for a quick equity liquidation often results in a lower sale price, acceptance of terms not favorable to you over the long term, commitment to a covenant-not-to-compete that is too restrictive, or even agreeing to help the purchaser and tying the sales price to future company performance. Perhaps equally important to these financially-related issues is the notion of purpose. If you leave without a plan, you run the very real risk of becoming disengaged and bored with life—right at the moment it's supposed to be fun again.

The decision to sell is as much art as it is a science. When do I sell my business? Who do I sell it to? Will they look after it, or will the purchaser rename it? What happens to my employees? Should I liquidate rather than sell? Can one of my children or family members take over for me? Should I still own a percentage of the business after I leave, or should I tie the sales price to some future performance? Should I agree to stay on for a while? These are just some of the issues on the pro and con list that must be considered.

When evaluating all the options, don't base these pros and cons on idealized opinions. Be honest with yourself so you can begin to see where the problems are. If, for example, your child or heir apparent just doesn't have the leadership ability to make your company work, this is something you need to realize early, especially if you're going to rely on an income from the company in future years.

Remember, you are predicting your future. It is fundamentally important that your current day bias does not influence your decision-making. You must think first in terms of yourself and what you want to do with your life once you sell because you don't get do-overs. Your expectations and needs ten years ago are not the same as they are today; and they will assuredly be different ten years from now. If you need to, pull in a confidant to discuss the realities of each issue affecting your business and your retirement. In many instances, business owners are simply too ingrained in the operations of their companies and cannot objectively assess the pros and cons of selling. Remember, you are seeking clarity in this step. A truthful perspective is what is needed. Remove your bias and look at your situation in the reality it exists in.

Step 4: Accepting the Truth

Business owners like to embellish the truth in order to make their companies look better than they are. This isn't immoral; it's salesmanship. In business, winners like winners, and your potential customers and clients have high expectations. So to grow sales, business owners tend to create an aura of success, even if some aspects of the business come nowhere close to this expectation.

Over time, the process of salesmanship could lead to a distorted view of what your business is actually good at. Too many business owners who have been in the game for a long time become somewhat disconnected from the daily, behind-the-scenes process of their business. They actually start to believe their anecdotal performance perspective is real, and they manage their company as though this is a reality. The truth, as they say, will set you free.

The issue of truthfulness has significant impact on the exit planning process. Although to this point we have focused much of the discussion on the interests of the business owner, the reality of truthfulness greatly influences your expectation of corporate value and sale price. How the company is efficiently operated, how it makes its product or performs its service, and who in the company controls the value of the business are all important truths to be acknowledged.

You have brought your company this far, but no matter what level of success you might have enjoyed, you are beginning to realize there is always a lot of work yet to be done. Truth is, if you do not understand the importance of defining an effective strategy that takes into account all conceivable issues affecting the sale and your exit, you're in big trouble.

This is the time for a strict rule: only the truth. Accurate figures, expectations, realities, problems, and solutions are what you need. You cannot afford to take the wrong step here. If your business needs some considerable work in order to be sold in five years time, then you have to admit this to yourself. It is not a failure on your part because now, for perhaps the first time, your true long-term priorities have changed.

The reality of the situation is that the exit strategy you never put in place is as much for your benefit as it is for the benefit of the company. You have to prepare yourself and your company for your exit. This could require some sacrifices on your part, because the business you have cherished all these years may simply not be attractive enough for someone to step up and buy it. It may have filled your life's plan, and you are no doubt proud of what you have accomplished, but if you are truthful with yourself about its value, then a few changes might be in order. In some cases, the addition of new employees in critical areas may be needed. Perhaps staff changes are needed so a new purchaser can see that you have the right person in the right job for the right reasons. Also, a lot of functional and financial improvement might be needed. Perhaps your accounts receivables are unbalanced, or your line of credit is maxed out. Maybe some of those financial reports your staff have been telling you about have yet to be finalized and issued on a routine basis. These are the types of things purchasers are going to want to see if they are going to consider your company.

Accept the truth and work toward a real, viable end goal. It would be a shame for you to think that your business is fine as it is and then leave a significant amount of cash or favorable terms on the table. An effective business exit strategy is based on truth and the reality of your situation—never forget that.

Step 5: Revising Your Short-Term Business Strategy

The next step in planning your exit starts with the end. By now you should be realizing you have to change your short-term business strategy. Most business owners contemplating an exit strategy make the fundamental mistake of focusing merely on the money aspect of the plan. They place incredible weight on how much their company is worth and how much of that they will put in their pocket. Yes, yes, yes, the money is important. But understand that the other half of the exit equation centers on you and your personal ambitions. Your personal time horizon, your health, your interests, and your lifestyle need to be considered as integral aspects of your exit strategy.

Consequently, Step 5 deals with your short-term business strategy that, when fully implemented, generates the exit velocity you need to escape the gravitational pull of your company. So, with this need in mind, let's focus on starting at the end. We start by first setting a time horizon for your exit. At first, this may seem unorthodox, but keep in mind the pendulum swing of your efforts—from focusing on the needs of the company to the recognition of your needs when it is time for you to leave. Having an exit date makes short-term planning easier because you can structure it along a timeline. Your time horizon is important because you need to give yourself, and your company, the time necessary to prepare for your exit.

Think of it in these terms; what happens to an organization when you take the most important person out of the equation? Inevitably, the company's relationship with its banker will change, so its ability to secure future financing will be impacted. Key customers and clients will become uneasy when forced to deal with someone other than you. How will the corporate philosophy change? When the new company management team—absent you—begins to take the company in a new direction, it will affect the philosophical direction of the company which, in turn, affects its finances, customer/client relations, and business development tactics. When you begin to realize your company will be different when you are gone, it becomes apparent that you need to prepare it for your departure because your money and your reputation will be affected if the exit plan is poorly planned and horribly executed.

Some of the areas that may need to be addressed include the financial structure of the company, the structure of your management team, a revision to your business development plan, and commitments to strategic alliances and vendor/supplier contracts. By recognizing how your company is perceived and dealt with when you are no longer there, the obviousness of developing a short-term strategy to prepare your company for your departure comes into focus.

You will also have to measure your new goals against the needs of your employees and the future "value" of the business. As long as the time between now and your departure is occupied with strategies based on sales and value growth, the outcome will be to your personal advantage. Make sure that if you're going to reinvest capital in your business, it pays off—not in future sales, but in terms of realized value within your time horizon.

If you have never paid much attention to goal setting before, now's the time. In a recent study, 80% of all business owners admitted that they don't keep track of business goals at all. Of that 80%, 77% had still not achieved their initial goal. Structure, planning, and goal setting should be your new mantra. Things need to start changing, and you need a roadmap to know where you are headed.

Step 6: Deciding on a Plan of Action

Once you have revised your core short-term goals, you can structure a real plan of action. Whether you choose to retire next year or in seven, short-term goals always feed into a long-term plan. Your long-term plan is to get out and get out happy. This means you need to gear up for the next few years of your business' life. Your plan of action will focus on creating value, defining corporate structure in your absence, and adherence to a sustained path toward profitable growth.

It may sound easy enough—but it is not. Chances are you have been running your business a certain way for many years, and it's worked out just fine. Truth be told, you might not even have any ideas on how you can improve the operational performance of your company.

Most business owners run their businesses on their gut feeling. Yes, there is something to be said for experience, but reliance on anecdotal evidence renders decisions that come too late to take effective action, and since the current economy is moving at a faster rate of speed than ever before, any delay in exercising the best judgment and strategy is surely going to be expensive.

That's why it always helps to talk to other business owners, industry professionals, analysts, or accountants. Business metrics can be an effective indicator of performance failures and strategy successes. But remember, metrics are of zero value if you do not take decisive action to correct problems identified by the data. When you start digging around, there are bound to be some new ideas waiting to be implemented.

If there was ever a time to be laser focused, it is now. The earlier you can pinpoint and devise a suitable plan of action, all while keeping the prize in focus (e.g., your successful exit), the sooner you can start making it work. That way, when the time comes to sell, you and your business will be prepared. Step 6 is about settling on a plan of action that will create business value that is saleable.

Step 7: Selling Your Business: The Time Value of Money Time vs. Rewards

As you begin to understand the critical nuances that

come with liquidating your equity holdings in your business and leaving with your money on your terms, Step 7 is the culmination of "letting go and winning big". If your heart is set on reaping the rewards of a lifetime's worth of work, selling your business is the last crucial step. The process you have just read about requires a lot of work on your part. The good news is this is the formative process of developing and implementing an educated, qualified exit strategy.

> **R**eview & balance your checkbook
>
> **E**valuate & differentiate needs from wants
>
> **W**eigh up pros and cons
>
> **A**ccept the truth
>
> **R**evise your short-term strategy
>
> **De**cide on a plan of action
>
> **S**ell your business

When you reach the last step—after you've made sure your business is the best that it can be before you sell—you'll enjoy complete peace of mind, knowing you've done all you can for your future. Now it is a race against time.

Time is always against you as a business owner. When you started out, you had dreams and plans, many of them that never saw fruition because of time constraints. Selling your business will be an emotional experience. It marks the end of a chapter of your life you will never get back. But if done correctly, great things are on the horizon for you.

Implementing a good business exit strategy is about time management. As your professional career comes to a close, it is important to understand it cannot be rushed or cobbled together because you're tired or because you are too stubborn to make the necessary changes. The amount of time you put into planning your exit strategy will directly affect the rewards you receive. But despite your time horizon and the inevitable hurdles you will face along the way, don't mistake preparation for duty. If you continue to sell yourself short by putting your ultimate end game on hold, chances are you will be the business owner who stayed too long, or didn't negotiate the best price, or agreed to stay on after you sold. To get REWARDS, you need to plan for them, despite what anyone else says. They are not going to accidentally fall into your lap.

Work will no longer be your source of income. Every cent you earn from the sale of your business will go toward your personal happiness. And for that reason alone, you need to take it seriously. Unless you plan on reinvesting in another venture, income as you know it will never be the same. Now, let's put it all in context. Chapter 1 was merely the overview of the process and the intricacies of what needs to be done if you want to leave your company with your money and on your terms. Remember, there are no do-overs.

The Basis of the Exit Plan

You know the clichés: you're unique, there's no one in the world quite like you, you went into business to do it your way, and so on. When it comes to your business, these are not clichés in as much as they are truisms. Your business is a delicate mixture of your needs, desires, and ideas brought to life. It is as much a part of you as your business is part of the market in which you compete. And because of that, there is no shelf-ready exit strategy that is right for any one individual, let alone you. For much of the same reasons you went into business for yourself, your exit strategy should not mirror the one used by a business associate, nor should it be so generic that one size fits all.

If you think for a minute that all exit strategies are created equal, you're wrong! This book and the message it presents is not the standard fair. Most business books on this subject tend to focus on how to establish the value of your business and then how to sell it. Admittedly, these topics are important, but believe it or not, they are not the most important issues facing a business owner who is readying himself and his business for separation. As it stands, your exit strategy needs to suit you and your situation. This is your custom exit strategy, and to get it right you'll need to learn a thing or two in this chapter.

Your Economic Countdown

Timing and its impact on the economy will play an important role in the eventual sale of your business. For the past few years, it has been a rocky ride for businesses all over America. We might have the largest economy in the world, but we have fallen from first to fourth in worldwide economic rank according to the *Global Competitiveness Report*. Since the economic collapse in 2008, there seems to be an economic crisis *du jour* that rears its ugly head every so often. Every time we seem to get some good news, something half way around the world tends to take our economic legs out from underneath us.

But truth be told, the recession is far from over. There is simply too much debt in the country and too much uncertainty as to how it will get fixed. As a result, the economy has maintained a death grip on the financial markets, holding it hostage in a spiraling black hole of instability. With pending tax hikes, growing inflation fears, and soaring energy and food prices—how can you plan against a continued economic meltdown?

Many of the talking heads seen on both the liberal and conservative talk shows are claiming the economic malaise we find ourselves in is not likely to remedy itself over the next few years. What we are seeing now is that many baby boomer-aged business owners are growing tired of the grind and simply do not want to put their ever dwindling asset base at risk. In short, they do not want to work harder for less and are finding themselves wondering if it is time to move on. You really can't blame them for their concerns. With business valuations plummeting and the market being flooded with small businesses for sale, no one is making money selling their business in this recession. The American economy is operating at the mercy of politicians, ever-changing social ideologies, and foreign government economic and austerity challenges. As they say, it's important to sell your business during a period of general economic stability; timing is everything.

Regardless of your political affiliation, the United States is navigating a complex time in our nation's history. Since the bursting of the real estate bubble in 2007, the economy as a whole has been ravaged by high unemployment, selective failure of the financial markets, economic bail-outs of big business and even bigger government behemoths (e.g., Fannie Mae and Freddie Mac), and ballooning federal deficits that have swallowed the term "billions" and has all of us wondering what comes after a "trillion"! Losses in the stock market and housing value declines have accelerated consumer concerns resulting in the thwarting of consumer spending. With some 70% of the American economy based on citizen consumption, consumer savings only exacerbate the economic downturn.

In recent months American businesses have lost trillions of dollars in market capitalization; our legislators have designed and implemented massive financial bailout plans; unemployment remains dauntingly high; and the number of business and residential foreclosures across the country continue to climb. According to the proclamations of our governmental and elected officials, the U.S. economy apparently hit rock bottom in 2009; but it certainly does not feel like it.

If you do not have the gumption to position your business for long-term success, the only plausible action is to liquidate. A small business owner who thinks they are immune to economic downturns or is ambivalent to the new start-up business down the street that may likely be their next competitor is in for a rude awakening. No small business in today's marketplace can survive on automatic pilot. Business owners must drive their businesses every day; because if you don't, you will soon lose your nest egg.

For those small business owners who see the horizon and are beginning to think about exiting their businesses, there are many questions at hand. What is your business worth? Can your business afford you to leave? What's the best way to sell your company? How do you get your money without being tied to your business forever? As business owners approach the end of their entrepreneurial careers, they start to realize that in order to create the wealth needed to be comfortable in their post-career years, the exit strategy they never gave much credence to is now critically important.

As the debt problem in America gets worse, its impact on the American dollar will greatly affect your profits and business valuation. If this happens, what will be your contingency plan? In one fell swoop, all of your hopes and dreams of financially benefiting from years of risk-taking could mean nothing.

The simple notion that competition, cash flow, marketing, and operational efficiency are the only hurdles facing small business owners each morning when they arrive at work is no longer valid. Fundamental shifts in how businesses are regulated, financed, taxed, and competed against now present a new normal.

As a business owner who has fought the good fight for some time now, the question is whether you want to fight the fight under these new terms. This is your economic countdown; and timing is everything. If you have had enough, you must plan your exit now and work diligently to put that plan into motion or risk walking away empty handed. Through no fault of your own, the American economy could ruin your retirement plans.

Yes, there is always the prospect that common sense will prevail and the economy and our national leaders will figure it out, but what are the chances of that happening? You've seen the news reports; common sense is not in the recipe. Add to this reality the underlying need for certainty, and you begin to better understand that every entrepreneur and business owner has serious concerns over what the future might bring. You need to make sure that now, more than ever, you start putting your future and financial independence on your to-do list.

Why an Exit Strategy?

In an article by Barbara Taylor, "Are Baby Boomers Ready to Exit Their Businesses[1]?", older workers who simply do not or can't retire appear to be on a collision course with a growing number of disgruntled and burned-out baby boomer-aged business owners who intend to sell their businesses and enter retirement.

According to Ms. Taylor, as of January 1, 2012, the oldest of America's Baby Boomer generation started turning 65 at a rate of 10,000 a day — a trend that will last for the next 19 years. A significant portion of these Baby Boomers who own small businesses want to sell their businesses because they simply do not want to continue fighting for less.

What is interesting is that both groups — senior citizens who want to work and business owners who don't want to work — find themselves the benefactor of their own poor planning.

While there is no shortage of articles proclaiming that people born from 1946 through 1964 are ill-prepared for

---

1 Taylor, Barbara. *The New York Times*. 10 Feb, 2011. <http://boss.blogs.nytimes.com/2011/02/10/are-baby-boomers-ready-to-exit-their-businesses/>

retirement, my assessment is that poor planning is prevalent in both groups. For seniors, the automatic-pilot management style of their stock portfolios and the assumption that double-digit growth was forever routine has them feeling uncomfortable as to their ability to make ends meet in retirement. In similar fashion, too many baby boomer-aged business owners have put off necessary exit planning until the eleventh hour to set a plan in place to sell their businesses and recover their wealth.

By some estimates as many as 75 percent of all business owners are afflicted with the no-exit-plan disease. According to a 2008 study conducted by Atlanta-based White Horse Advisors and Vistage International, 96 percent of baby boomer-aged business owners agreed that having an exit strategy was important—but 87 percent did not have a written plan.

The problem with poor exit planning is that its risks are generally innocuous until it is time to leave; then the reality of the situation is simply too much to overcome. At issue in the coming years is timing: lack of planning and a glut of supply. With 15 million small businesses across the country owned by boomers, the sheer number of businesses expected to come onto the market is staggering. Current statistics show 9 million of America's 15 million business owners were born in or before 1964, resulting in one business owner turning 65 every 57 seconds. As suggested by Ms. Taylor, there is a potential for a tsunami of businesses for sale in the very near future.

Despite the challenges of the day, chances are you've just about reached that point in your life when the importance of an exit strategy is becoming more obvious. But we're not talking about just any plan; we're talking about a plan that accounts for the issues you cannot control. When you really think about it, your exit strategy needs to be able to predict the future. This is an adapt-or-die situation.

Think back to those glorious days when you worked your ass off. Remember the first time you had some real money in your pocket? How you poured your blood, sweat and tears into making your business run like a well-oiled machine? It was exciting, terrifying, and inspiring all at once. Formulating an exit strategy is no different. In fact, I would argue that leaving your business is far more important than the day you started it. No doubt, you have more to lose now than you did when you opened the doors. And because of the realities of your success, the plan you never really gave much credence to is the most important assignment you will ever face in your professional career.

We start the process at the end and work backwards. Now this may seem a little unorthodox at first glance, but we can't go about creating a plan if we do not know how we will gauge success.

Here are some things to think about.

- Why do you want to sell your company?
- What is your time horizon for leaving?
- How do you want to leave your company?
- What will you do when you leave?
- What kind of money do you need?

A good plan is born from knowing yourself and your company. If you are going to bridge the gap between operating your company now and successfully leaving it at the time of your choosing, you're going to need some introspection and will need to put forth a lot of hard work. There is a general misconception among small business owners that leaving your company is easy. This is simply not true.

By selling your business, you'll have the money and time to do things that you've always dreamed of doing. This prospect is exciting; however, the loss of purpose and social connections that come with being a business owner could leave you feeling unfulfilled and empty once you leave. When you factor in the loss of salary and the reality of having to pay for some of the perks and daily expenses your company used to pay for you, you begin to understand the intricacies of the exit equation. So, before making such a huge decision, you need to take the time to determine what's right for you.

Here are some important considerations to keep in mind as you start to formulate your exit strategy:

1. What makes you happy?

One of the biggest reasons we become unhappy is that we fall out of sync with our personal values. The reason we got into business in the first place might not be the best reason to stay in business over the long term. Some entrepreneurs like to start a business, and once it is up and running, they get bored. Other entrepreneurs struggle through the start-up process, only to hit their stride when it's time to really start to grow and optimize the business. Staying too long or leaving too quickly may be a significant mistake. To make matters worse, too many business owners lose their individualism; their business becomes their identity, and everything they do is based on some business need. Could it be that staying in your business becomes a life-avoidance strategy? For too many, running your business becomes something you do because you don't know what else you would do. If you tell me running your business makes you happy, I will tell you have lost touch with what is important in life.

2. Go to a class reunion

Chances are that when you were younger you never saw the value in going to a class reunion. You can only take so many bullshit stories in any given evening, and reunions tend to be classic examples of one-upmanship. But if you are thinking it may be time to leave your company, my suggestion is to go to one of your class reunions and see if one of your classmates is doing something you are envious of. If so, it may be a sign you would enjoy doing something else. Jealousy has a positive spin if it is used constructively.

3. Confront your demons

Too many of us have excuses for just about everything.

- "I was going to start an exercise program but…"
- "I always wanted to go to Australia but …"
- "I knew something was wrong with my health but…"

If you sell your business, you won't be able to use time or money as an excuse any more. You might actually accomplish something for yourself by ditching the comfortable excuses.

4. Think about yourself

For many business owners, their business gives them a deep sense of purpose. If the business benefits, then you benefit; at least that is the conventional thinking for almost all business owners But if you sell your company, you need to refocus your sense of purpose. This is a critical issue and one many business owners struggle with when they leave their companies.

5. Imagine your post-sale life in detail

You need to understand that your life without your company is exceptionally difficult to comprehend, let alone get used to. Your days are not likely to be scripted at first, but eventually you will get there. You will begin to realize how much money you really spend, and for the first time in a long time, you will be spending your own money. Your acquaintances will change as your past business friends continue to let their companies run their lives and you look for something constructive to do to fill the time void. You will find a new passion; you will get things done because there is no one to delegate to.

It is not an easy thing to do — to imagine your life after selling your equity stake. But much like writing a business plan, start playing a few "what-if" games. This level of detail helps you get clarity on how you will come to enjoy your post-sale life.

As you can begin to see, there are personal and external factors that will help you form a strategic list of criteria that will help you achieve your goal of leaving your company with your money and on your terms. Take into account every aspect of your life and how it will or might change after you have sold your business. Once all of these issues are tabulated and assessed, you will create the clarity needed to formulate an effective exit strategy. When complete, you won't simply rely on a mixed bunch of wishes and expectations. You will understand the keys to your future happiness.

Succession Depression: Handing Over the Reigns

It is very common for a son or a daughter to go into the family business once they have come of age. In the 1950s this was most evident with the barbershops and grocery stores titled "Hamilton and Son," or something similar. Although not as commonplace today, there are instances and times for a business owner to leave their business in the capable hands of their kin or someone who they have been working with for years.

If you are thinking of succession instead of sale—or succession as part of a sale—this can be a very trying time for you. How exactly do you hand over the reins of your business to someone who isn't you? No one understands how much time, effort, and hard work goes into keeping your business afloat better than you do. Now you have to give this responsibility to someone new. Here are your options!

Offer your business to your management team in a choreographed buyout. This way you will still be able to sell your business for top dollar and will rest easy knowing it's in the hands of people you know and care about. It's also more likely to continue succeeding if your managers have a direct hand in it.

Can you sell your business to a family member? Technically you can, but we all know this is not always the case. Transferring the ownership of your company to a family member comes steeped in trouble, so you need to do it right. Sit down with your intended successor and discuss their plans. Give them a proposed timeline, and make sure they understand the conditions of the transfer.

If you're not going to sell your business to them but just have them operate it for you, then the business will still need to pay you a "salary" or "pension". There are some pitfalls to being an absentee owner.

Then there is the outside sale. Although more difficult to gain traction than the comfort of an internal sale, there are advantages. We will discuss all of these options later in this book.

As part of your introspective thoughts, think carefully about your choices. Regardless of how you do it, in the end you will need the financial rewards necessary to live your life away from your company. The money is yours, so come to grips with what you need to be happy.

Shooting From the Hip Does Not Work

As the economy continues to suffer, aging baby boomer business owners are in a quandary about what to do next.

On the one hand, you're not ready to retire. The stock market is not exactly steaming along, so the adverse impact it has made to your retirement nest egg is significant, or at the very least, your retirement dollars are not growing at the rate of growth you had projected was necessary for you to retire on your terms. Similarly, you find yourself knee-deep in various business initiatives to keep your company afloat as Washington dilly-dallies around fighting amongst themselves as to who can come up with the dumber plan. As they play games, the economy suffers, as does your bottom line. Consequently, your business probably needs cash to keep its corporate mission in sight. But more cash means more risk for you.

In a recent article by John Melloy, "Boomer Dilemma: Delay Retiring or Take on More Risk[2]?" this issue is brought into perspective. Granted, the referenced article centers on stock market performance and whether Baby Boomers should put off retiring or adopt a riskier strategy that generates higher yields,

---

2 Melloy, John. 17 Aug, 2011. <http://www.cnbc.com/id/44176235/Boomer_Dilemma_Delay_Retiring_Or_Take_On_More_Risk>

but this notion also applies to baby boomer-aged business owners as they struggle through the current economic crisis.

There is no secret formula or magic pill to discern what to do next. Every small business owner is faced with different challenges, changing conditions, personal interests, and market competition. To make matters unnecessarily complicated, many small business owners typically put their companies and employees' interests ahead of their own. Many of you are spending too much time working in your business rather than working on your business; and we all know this is a recipe for disaster.

Successful small business owners drive their businesses. At the end of the day is it fair to you and your family to further risk your equity by trying to keep your company in business, or is it time for you take what is left of your equity and enjoy it?

Experts predict 90% of all baby boomer-aged business owners won't plan an exit strategy. The result—business owners are forced to give their companies away or liquidate for pennies on the dollar. What do you have to do to prep your business for sale? How long do you think selling your business will take? Herein lies the trap. Often the sale of a good business can take several months, even years to consummate. Perhaps even more important is the preparation process. Not all businesses can be sold as-is. No doubt you think your business is worth something; probably a lot. In reality, your business is not worth what you think it is. *Why?* Because you have probably built and operated your business to serve your personal needs or your management style. While this serves your ego, it does little to create true value.

This reality needs to be factored into your exit plan.

Buyers come in all shapes and sizes. Some are premium buyers because you have something strategic they want; whether it is a geographic market, a complimentary product or service, an economy-of-scale, a particular client/customer, or a profit they are willing to pay for. Others might include a loyal lieutenant who wants the opportunity to sit in the big chair, or even a competitor down the street that wants what you have. Maybe your son or daughter wants to run the family business. Buyers want your business for some reason; your challenge is to find out what that reason is and exploit it to your advantage.

You need to see the sale through the eyes of your buyer. If the business does better with you in it, a buyer will request that you stick around for a while to ensure a smooth, successful transition. That "awhile" might take years. Maybe the buyer wants you to leave right away and requests a discount for cash. Perhaps your buyer does not have all the capital necessary to meet your selling price and asks you to carry some, or all, of the note. Planning early and being prepared to exercise the best option for you while maintaining a realistic valuation is the key to every exit strategy.

Imagine not having a plan, staying too long, and then deciding to sell your business. Too many Baby Boomers will find themselves in this predicament because their egos get in the way. They will come to the realization too late to maximize the value of their equity and leave on their terms.

Implementing a real exit plan means covering all of your bases. It's about addressing all the details you have repeatedly put off in lieu of more important business. The concept of retirement or the thought that someday you will leave your business is, in and of itself, not a plan. In business, timing is everything. Whether you are a maker of widgets, the purveyor of great suggestions and ideas, or the supplier extraordinaire, your successes are as much a function of timing as they are of hard work. So how is your exit strategy different? It shouldn't be!

When you start the planning process for your exit you are, in essence, creating time. By creating a plan and implementing its commensurate strategies, you have created the time which may be necessary to take advantage of an opportunity that would otherwise not be noticeable to you because you are not looking for your exit. Taking positive steps to structure your exit might present you with alternative options. The market might be ripe for the sale of your business earlier than you planned. Perhaps by structuring an exit strategy you find that one of your lieutenants shows an interest in acquiring your equity because he can see that you are serious about leaving. And it is certainly possible that an exit plan, if done correctly and with purpose, results in you making key decisions that aid the growth of your bottom line. The key is to orientate yourself in this plan before you run out of options. Spend real time preparing for success, just like you did at the beginning of your career. This is often the missing ingredient for many business owners.

In order to do achieve what seems to be impossible, you simply have to start. You need to come to the realization of what's important to you; what you want to do next in your life; how you will pay for it; and how you will be happy. All great business exit strategies take time and early planning. That's why this book is called *The Exit Equation* and not *Sell Your Business*. I am intent on giving you the insight and perspective needed to implement a successful strategy and avert your biggest mistake.

The Emotional Tug of War

Perhaps you have been giving this whole notion of establishing an exit strategy some thought for awhile now, or maybe you have never pursued it because it seemed so far off and you knew in your heart you weren't ready to do it. Regardless of your position on the subject, we hope you are now beginning to recognize the need and the process. But as you begin to warm to the idea that planning your work and working your plan makes sense, you come to a crashing realization — one that is difficult to overcome in terms of loyalty and virtue. Welcome to the uncomfortable position of picking you and your family over the employees and company that has delivered success..

Think of the excitement you will feel when, following a ton of planning and implementing, you can see the end of the rainbow. And yes, just like all the fairy tales, this rainbow has a pot of gold waiting for you. The cash is tangible; it is the culmination of years of sweat equity, risk-taking, and perseverance. he money is yours to do as you please. Take a trip, buy a boat, build a cabin, live life to the fullest. The check isn't heavy, but the commas are nice to see. The money is all yours. It feels really good!

Now think of the expression in the eyes of your employees the day you tell them you have sold the business. How do you think they will feel? Betrayed, helpless, perhaps overwhelmed with a deep uneasiness because they do not know what this means to them. Sure, they will be happy for you and will smile and say congratulations. But deep down, after they walk back to their workstations or spin around in their chairs to get back to work, they will start to feel uneasy. Why? Because their lifeblood and safety net will be gone; announcing to the world that there is something better out there and they want to go and get it. The company and the employees become secondary, and everyone on your staff will feel the hurt. And if you are any semblance of a real person, one who has taken great pride to do the right thing for his company and its workforce, you will feel the same sadness. This is the emotional tug-of-war that affects almost every business owner who says, "show me the money."

This is the art of the sale. If you have sold a business before, then you know what you're in for. Most business owners haven't, and this can prove to be a stressful, tense time for everyone—staff included. After all they have done for you, you want to know in your heart of hearts that their jobs will be safe. They are be part of the deal right; you have negotiated their continued livelihood. They want to believe you.

When the end is near, you will be brimming with emotions—and that tug on your heart will start. You likely will feel sad, traitorous, or even angry with yourself for abandoning something so close to you. These are emotions you need to expect so that you can master them when they happen. If they sneak up on you, you could lose your nerve and let the opportunity pass by.

There are many ways you could end up selling your business. Choose partial or full sale, immediate or phased payment, or simply liquidate your assets. Any of these options work provided they are harmonious with your exit plan. When you balance the plan with reality and take into account the accuracy of your intentions regardless of the emotions and second-guessing you are likely to endure, you can leave your company forever and feel good about it. That's the rarity you want to achieve.

When your business hits the market, your tug of war will begin. It will be a battle trying to remain true to the convictions you've designed for yourself—but you must do it. Do not take your eyes off the prize, because in the end, everyone comes out a winner. You, your money, and they employees you have left behind will fend for themselves like they always have. Don't lose the tug-of-war.

Averting Your Greatest Regret

Although building your company for sale is the *right* mindset, it is understood this wasn't your primary ambition when you started in business. Maybe you were cursed with incompetent bosses in your life, or you had an opportunity to buy a business you knew how to improve. Maybe you just had something in you that other people do not. Regardless of the reasons, most entrepreneurs have the innate ability to assemble resources, find and manage capital, and rally the troops to take a vision, an idea, and move it from a thought to a reality. It is a building process; building systems, marketing networks, and confidence to do what was once only dreamed. You probably entered the business ownership world because you wanted more freedom, more money, and the chance to shape your own career.

As a business consultant intent on helping businesses get better, I have laid witness to a very unfortunate trend that is as startling as it is baffling. Too many small business owners have simply forgotten the formula they used to start and grow their businesses. Remember the days when you started your business? You prepared yourself emotionally and financially, committing constant attention to the process. You were eager to be successful and exemplified that can-do attitude that often was a difference maker, especially when times got tough. But now you find yourself in a tough spot, and you're scared, mad, and confused.

I continue to proclaim that business owners can either bury their heads in the sand hoping any economic downturn spares them, or they can do something about it. Someone who I know is doing something about that. Bill is a small business owner and has been for the last 21 years. He is well-read, insightful, and mad. He is mad about the situation the country finds itself in and the position from which his company must now compete. You see, Bill's concerns are not of his doing because he has not stood still in an economy that has too many small business owners cowering and complaining.

Bill has accepted the challenge of putting his business in a position of strength. He continues to focus his efforts and that of his staff on three critical areas of improvement (service, value, and competitive position) that he believes will make all the difference. He has gone back to his entrepreneurial roots in order to succeed.

Back when you entered the business market, you had a motive and a mission. For many small business owners, they all answered the following questions ("How to Decide if Entrepreneurship Is Right for You."[3] *The Wall Street Journal*):

1. Am I passionate about my product or service? To simply survive and then to grow your business you had to have the desire to get through the rough times, even when your enthusiasm was severely tested.
2. What is my tolerance for risk? There was no guarantee of a paycheck; you had to work hard for your money, and you had to take risks.

---
[3] Debaise, Colleen. How to Decide if Entrepreneurship Is Right for You. 21 Sep, 2009. <http://online.wsj.com/article/SB125354895752528171.html>

3. Am I good at making decisions? No one else was going to do it for you. Your success or demise was your own doing.
4. Am I willing to take on numerous responsibilities? There was no one to delegate to; you had to learn as much as you could about everything all the time.
5. Will I be able to avoid burnout? You were hell-bent on succeeding, and the business climate back then didn't make excuses.

Bill understood these issues and took his business back in time. He has spent considerable energy redesigning, restructuring, and reinventing his business. Some may look at Bill as being naive; some may think he's foolish. I have come to know Bill, and he is neither. He is now planning his exit.

I know what you are thinking: how do I run my profitable business and implement a strategy where I walk away from it? It is a dichotomy that business owners struggle to balance. But you cannot underestimate the power of a focused mindset.

Remember the early days? Everything you did revolved around your business. Family vacations were dictated by payroll and dinner out with your spouse always seemed to include a potential client sitting at another table in the restaurant you just had to say hello to. You had less freedom and less money and fought to keep your business afloat. Then, for whatever reason, things settled down and business started to come to you. You learned to delegate; you made better decisions; you hired with a keener insight; and you really started to understand the economic drivers of your business. This is the growth curve for many businesses and their owners. You had to fight for your business each step of the way, and that's why leaving it is so hard.

Do you have debt? How much tax will you have to pay on the sales price? Do most of your customers only deal with you? What about health insurance; how does this huge expense get covered every month? The questions are only just beginning to come into focus for you. This seems like a monumental task—a definite game changer. And let's not forget about the time element and the amount of effort it will take to exit the right way. But this is your future we're talking about, something that you have successfully put off for too long. Your mindset and expectations need to change before an exit strategy can be fully understood and your plan can gain traction.

Your retirement can be extraordinary, and you deserve to pull out on your terms with your money. Family and friends will try to influence this decision. They will question you as to why you are considering walking away from your business. They will argue you have too much to give up. But if their comments and personal opinions jeopardize your prize, you have to put your foot down. True wealth, your wealth, comes from the sale of your business. You've worked for decades, and you understand what it takes to stay in the game and the risks you run if you stay too long. To get nothing at the end of all you have done and accomplished leads to depression and regret. You don't want to enter your twilight years feeling like half the person you once were.

This is the time for you to reclaim your youth. Your children are gone. Work is over. You can finally do whatever makes you happy. A fulfilled career comes from careful planning, and you have accomplished this goal thus far. But you are not done; your mission is not complete. It is time to plan the next phase of your career. It's time to be selfish again or risk much of what you have built. It is time to get on with living.

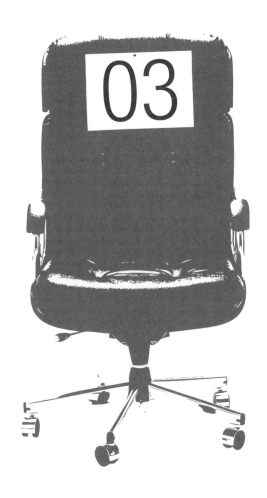

Plan Your Work and Work Your Plan

In the early 80s, I worked with a great guy named Joe. Joe's professional career was that of a planner/scheduler for an electric utility company. His job was to determine how best to build a coal-fired power plant, one piece at a time. I was a young, snotty-nosed college graduate who wanted to do things right, so I figured I better listen to Joe.

As my years working with Joe passed, he often made the same comment when giving advice: "plan your work and work your plan; with planning good things happen." It was Joe's mantra. He was good at it, and he was successful, so I took his advice.

Over the years, I have learned to be a planner and a scheduler. Whether I was saving for my first house, trying to balance a full-time job with a full night school schedule, or determining how best to build my businesses, I have used Joe's advice countless times to my advantage. The key to successful planning and scheduling, however, is to collect all the necessary information and assess it realistically. Determine what the impediments will be and how best to overcome them. You must also be able to quantify your personal limitations as well and retain the expertise you need to keep your success planning on track. Lastly, you have to be resilient, never letting anything or anyone get in your way.

In my opinion, there is not a goal, a dream, or a process that will not be accomplished if you simply "plan your work and work you plan." So when you think it is time to leave your company, your success will be solely determined by your ability to properly and effectively plan your departure and then stay on schedule to achieve the goal.

As an entrepreneur, you no doubt think you can do it yourself, but odds are you may struggle. This chapter of *The Exit Equation* will help you begin to understand the nuances of planning your work and working your plan because that's when good things happen.

Remember, success is always planned, it does not just happen; that's called luck, and you can't put luck in your bank account.

With Planning, Good Things Happen

The mistake far too many business owners make is to wait too long to sell their business. They hesitate, perhaps consumed in the day-to-day, and forget that their dream was to make money and then enjoy the elusive freedom they foresaw so many years ago. Or they have an unrealistic vision of walking into the sunset on selling day having decided to sell just a few weeks before to a buyer willing to give them everything they wanted on a plate. It would be nice if life worked like that, wouldn't it? Unfortunately, I'm here to tell you that it very rarely does.

Don't make the mistake of thinking your company will be easier to sell than it was to set up in the first place. It takes six to 12 months to typically sell a business that is already prepped and ready; the process itself once you have a buyer is likely to take months just to consummate the due diligence. The Letter of Intent, contract negotiations leading up to the Purchase Agreement, financing, etc., don't just happen overnight. Finding the right buyer can take even longer, and any little setback could land you right back at square one.

If you're putting off the sale of your company, perhaps because of loyalty to your employees or the fear of the great retirement unknown, you need to think long and hard about the ramifications of your decision. Waking up one day and deciding you've had enough doesn't work if you want all your money.

The obvious concern for any business owner who simply waits too long and does not adequately prepare himself and the company for their departure is the risk of not being able to sell it. What do I mean by that? Am I really saying that you can't sell your business when you desperately want to? Not necessarily. However, the fact is that if you wait until you really want or *need* to sell—perhaps you're exhausted by the daily demands of your company, you need money to fund the next stage of your life, or your spouse is putting pressure on you to spend retirement with the family—I guarantee you that, while you may be *able* to sell, you'll be leaving money on the table.

At some point, when you reach exhaustion from the years of pressure to keep your company going, you'll be so ready to walk away that you'll accept the first offer that comes along, perhaps taking as little as 40% or 50% cash up front from the cash proportion of your sale. It may sound unrealistic now, but the temptation to take the first offer that frees you will be overwhelming.

I am beginning to see this in my consulting business. Years ago when the economy was vibrant, business owners could put off the formation of an exit strategy and not suffer because of it. Back then there were plenty of opportunities to sell. Everyone was making money, and the merger and acquisition business was flush. This is not true any longer. With so many businesses owned by aging Baby Boomers coming onto the market, the opportunity to score big despite a lack of planning is gone. You will now find yourself and your business being just one of far too many businesses owned by aging Baby Boomers who want out. The glut will be tremendous and, if you are akin to the simple laws of supply and demand, you will be but a speck in the sandbox full of business sellers as buyers get the pick of the litter.

So don't be so damned naïve. Put yourself in a better position. Don't forget why you set up your company in the first place. It was your passport to freedom; you took control of your life early on in order to put yourself in the best position for retirement. Whether you picture retirement sitting on a beach, still doing some work at home, traveling, or just spending more time with your loved ones, your company was going to be your way to do anything you wanted. The money you'd make from selling it when the time was right was going to fund your lifestyle and give you the freedom you'd need to truly enjoy the rest of your life.

Keep this in mind, especially when your emotions get the better of you and you can't see how you could leave the business you created and grew from scratch. As you continue to spend far too much time behind your desk, and you are growing tired of it, remind yourself that your company is merely a means to a perfect end.

Create a Timetable to Leave Your Company – 3 to 5 Years

In an ideal world, you would have had potential exit strategies in mind when you first set up your business. If you didn't, however, you're certainly not alone. Many new business owners throw themselves enthusiastically into setting up their first business, never thinking of how they will get out of it at the end.

As the owner, I'm willing to bet that it's your energy that keeps your business on track, brings in those new clients, and finds those key sales. You are the strategist; you keep your staff on their toes. So what happens once you get tired of the chase and you simply run out of gas? If instead of spending your days chasing down new sales leads, you'd rather just have some down time, what is the impact on your company? Perhaps even more importantly, how will you feel if you can't take your foot off the gas pedal?

What happens is the company stagnates and success (and profits) starts to erode. Employees begin to exercise a bit more freedom in their work hours and their performance. Eventually your management team makes some decisions that adversely affect the company. Suddenly your company isn't looking as attractive to buyers as it maybe was just a couple of years ago — all because you have taken your foot off the gas pedal. In truth, most companies cannot run on auto-pilot. When you get tired, the company suffers; that's what I mean I say, "you've left it too late."

This is why it's important to plan ahead and get out before you really *need* to. You don't want to be left with a company that is worth less and have no exit strategy in sight; that's the end to your retirement hopes and dreams.

My advice to you is to start the planning process. Don't wait too long and find yourself and your company decaying from the inside out.

The planning process varies by company and company owner but in many circumstances three to five years *before* you want to sell is the key to the sale. Start making plans while your enthusiasm and energy is still strong; that gusto and passion may be what sells your company in the first place. Taking the longer term view also gives you time to consider how best to transfer your wealth, thus minimizing any tax liability.

Planning for your exit early allows you to get your business into the best possible shape to sell. A positive side effect is that it also encourages you to identify your own personal and financial goals and look at how you can achieve the hopes and ambitions you had for your future so long ago.

Planning ahead forces you to choose a milestone at which you want to sell your company; it may be a particular year (perhaps you want to retire at 65, so will need to start considering your exit strategy at 60) or a certain level of sales or profit. You could also look ahead at external forces that may influence your company's production, sales, supply, competitiveness, and bottom line in the future.

Look at what is happening in your sector of the market: is it growing, consolidating? What does that mean for your company in the long term? What are your competitors doing, and will you be able to stay ahead of technological developments in your industry? You want to sell your company while it is still growing profits and has potential to grow them even further; if you're worried you won't be able to keep up with the market, you may want to plan your exit strategy earlier rather than later, before it becomes apparent to potential buyers as well.

Preparing your exit strategy so far ahead also enables you to really consider which succession option is best for your own personal financial goals; do you want to sell the company to an outsider, consider a management buy-out, or hand it over to offspring or other family members?

By planning early, you now have the time to evaluate all your options logically, calmly, and productively. If you decide you want to hand the business over to your children, for instance, you can use these three to five years to ensure they have the knowledge they need to succeed, sharing your insights, wisdom, and skills to make sure the company and its employees will be in safe hands once you retire.

If you do want to sell, planning ahead will allow you to consider your options and any bids for your company carefully, making sure you are really getting out of it what you put in. It will give you the time and the strength of purpose to say no to the wrong deals and to chase the right ones. If you're not in a hurry to sell immediately, potential buyers won't sense desperation and try to take advantage of you during negotiations. Don't forget, if handled right, this sale could be the gateway to an entirely new life. You owe it to the hard work you put into the company to make sure you walk away with enough to begin that new life with ease.

There's another bonus to starting to prepare to sell your business three to five years before you need to and that's to allow you to prepare all the financial information and other details you need to sell. This information is important as it presents a clearer perspective on your company's potential and will be what any new buyer wants to see. It's much easier to consistently compile these records over time than it is to have to rush to do it in the months before you want to sell.

The key to successful succession and exit planning is to think of it as a longer-term, tailored process that gives you the time to do your own due diligence and to really search inside yourself to understand what you want and need from this sale.

You only get the chance to do it once, so let's make sure that you get enough from it to set your retirement free.

Taking the Baby Steps

Once you have set a time horizon that allows sufficient time to get your company in order, you need to begin the process of formulating, compiling, assessing, and reporting the critical issues that will affect your sales price and the process of your exit.

Although we will delve into these issues in more detail in later chapters, here is a summary of some of the "baby steps" you need to begin to focus on:

Valuation

Despite the arguments from your accountant, determining the value of a business is more art than science. Several methods commonly used in calculating the value of a business include:

1. Multiplier or market valuation. This valuation method calculates value using an "industry average" sales figure as a multiplier. There are also a number of derivatives to this calculation, including average monthly gross sales, monthly gross sales plus inventory, or after tax profits of comparable businesses in the industry. For example, the seller of a business with annual sales of $250,000 may peg the multiplier at 1.50 to generate a sales price of $375,000 (e.g., $250,000 X 1.50 = $375,000).

It is important to note the difficulty in substantiating multipliers. Geographic area, economic conditions, company size, and diversity of sales can arguably affect the multiplier used.

2. Asset Valuation. Some businesses are worth no more than the value of their tangible assets. If a company is asset-intensive, such as retail businesses and manufacturing companies, you can use asset valuation as a means of determining corporate value. The goal of the seller in using this approach is to get the best possible price for their equipment, inventory, and other assets of the business. This method employs the following factors:

- Fair market value of fixed assets and equipment, or the price you would pay to purchase the assets or equipment;
- Leasehold improvements, or modifications to space that would be considered part of the property if you were to sell it or not renew a lease;
- Owner benefit, or the seller's discretionary cash for one year; and/or
- Inventory, including raw materials, work-in-progress, and finished goods or products.

3. Capitalized Earnings. This valuation method is suitable for service companies and other non-asset intensive businesses. Because these types of businesses see their greatest assets get up from their desks and go home each day, it is difficult to determine a value. The formula used to determine capitalized earnings is:

Projected Earnings/Capitalization Rate = Price

Where normal earnings are used to estimate projected earnings and capitalization rate is an estimated risk level of investing in the business compared with other investment instruments such as stocks or bonds.

The capitalization rate is an average of several factors, and may include length of time the company has been in business, length of time the current owner has owned the business, reasons for selling, risk factors, profitability, location, barriers to entry and exit, level of competition, industry potential, technology, and others.

4. Intangible Value (commonly known as goodwill). For those businesses that are not asset-intensive, its value may be harder to quantify. Professional service companies are examples of businesses that rely on its collective goodwill to establish its value.

For example, the Internal Revenue Service allows the use of an Excess Earnings Value to help define the value of these types of businesses. This process could look like this:

Net Income Before Tax

Add Back Normalization Adjustments
(Discretionary expenses)
= Normalized Net Income Before Taxes

Less Normalized Income Taxes
= Normalized Net Income After Taxes

Less Normal Return on Fixed Assets
= Excess Earnings

Divide by Capitalization Rate
= Goodwill Factor

Add Stockholders Equity
= Corporate Value

5. Return on Investment. The most common form of determining the value of a business is through its return on investment, or the amount of money the buyer will realize from the performance of the business. Although these values vary, industry experts define a good buy if the business can provide a return on the cash investment of 15 percent or more.

Severability

Although your direct involvement and hands-on efforts are great for your company and probably are the difference maker in how your company performs, prospective purchasers are not akin to having such a concentrated focus on business operations. If you are an owner who is involved in many aspects of your business, now is the time to start the process of disassociating yourself from being the focal point of the company. The issue here is one of sustainability; how will the company cope (e.g., customer loyalty, staff performance, flexibility of subcontractors and vendors) if your business orbits around you and the company changes hands? Now is the time to begin the process of assigning responsibility and allow your staff to earn all of their salaries. Buyers want a company that is resilient and not overly dependent on any one person. My minimal suggestion is to create an organizational chart, put a name in every box and assign responsibility, and start to structure your company and its operations to be consistent with the organizational chart. Most importantly, your name should only appear once on the chart and that's at the top.

Sustainability

You have been the keeper to your kingdom; everything the company has done has been under your guidance and tutelage. As you know, the view (and responsibility) while sitting in the big chair is different. It's challenging, scary, and frustrating all at the same time, but you have learned to master it, and it is now part of your character. You have collected great wisdom that comes from the experience having made good and bad decisions along the way. You, more than anyone else in your company, understand that knowledge is king. This is a critical understanding of the nuance of occupying the big chair. But as you begin to contemplate a transition for both you and your company, you have to begin the transfer of this knowledge to your staff so the company can achieve its full value. The due diligence process likely to be employed by a prospective purchaser often includes conversations with key staff members. The buyer is looking for a level of comfort knowing the key staff members can help the buyer sustain the operation during the initial months following the sale. If much of the knowledge is retained by you, the full value of the firm will not be realized in the sale price.

Reputation

Consider also your company's image and reputation. Look at your business from the perspective of the potential buyer. As you know, reputation in business is synonymous with success on many fronts. How you have treated your employees, vendors, clients, and your competition is an intrinsic value driver of your business.

These issues impact your bottom line, both now and post-sale. The better a potential buyer thinks of your company, the more money he or she will be prepared to hand over. Remember, the process of preparing your company for sale will require the owner to change the way the company looks, acts, and is perceived. You have to start moving the company away from your management style to one that is best suited for sale. This is one of the hardest things for a business owner to understand and achieve. Our egos get in the way because we view the company as still "ours" when in fact we really need to remove our bias from the business operation.

Assignment

The sale of your company will not occur in a vacuum, so begin the process of establishing a transition plan for everything from building rent and company financing, to client contract assignments and assumption of vendor services. Some of these efforts are designed to make the transition to a new owner smoother, while some are to ensure the sale can be consummated without any glitches. For instance, make sure your client contracts are assignable so the value of your work-in-process can be included in the sale price. What if you lease or own the building your company operates from? Make sure the lease can be transferred or make sure the rent your company pays you is defined for a reasonable term and/or is not subsidized by you, thus inflating or deflating the net value of your business. Likewise, making sure your bank financing for your current operation can be easily and effectively terminated upon a sale will give you the peace of mind needed to make the transition into retirement more rewarding.

Attractiveness

In a former profession as an environmental consultant, I always told my clients that if something looked bad, it was bad. Contrarily, if it looked good, it was good. Perception is the reality in many things in life, so take the time to look at your business from the outside. What does your logo look like? Are your corporate vehicles well maintained and attractive?

Do your employees dress appropriately How do you conduct business? What do your corporate e-mails look like? Are your office grounds well-maintained? Are the offices cluttered, or do they have a professional appearance? How does your staff answer the phone? Are they personable, helpful, and considerate? These issues may seem minor to you, but they are more of the intrinsic issues that help drive interest and value. Remember, your business currently suits you and your lifestyle needs, but this focus now needs to change. As you prepare your business for sale, you need to be interested in what a prospective buyer needs.

In the end, if it looks good, it is good!

Performance

Time to sort fact from fiction. Deep down, under the hardened layers of hard work, resiliency, and experience, most business owners have a soft underbelly of compassion and thoughtfulness. Whether it is the local United Way, a pancake breakfast fundraiser, or volunteering of labor or equipment for the local civic event, business owners are giving. But there is a reasonable limit, and even the most compassionate business owner has a line that cannot be crossed.

As you prepare your business for sale, consider the employees who you have graciously "looked the other way" for who have been allowed to keep their salaries despite excessive baggage and/or limited performance. Every company has these fictional performers on their staff, but as you begin to prepare your company for sale, the time has come to catapult these baggage clerks from the confines of your business. Yes, anytime you let someone go, it's hard; and yes, it has an impact on your remaining staff. However, it should be noted that the impact is not what you think. In many instances, letting an under-performing employee go does not necessarily create an uneasy feeling amongst remaining staff. In most cases, the remaining employees will actually have more respect for you when you make an obvious decision. So as you prepare your company for sale, now is the time to restructure your company for performance,

Documentation

In the end, documentation is icing on the cake. Prepare to document any patents or proprietary information; ensure your tax and official records, such as profit and loss statements, tax returns, leases, loans, accounts payable, and accounts receivable are up to date. If you do not have employment agreements for your staff, now is the time to fill that gaping hole. Update your business development databases and client files. These will be needed to support the due diligence process of the buyer. Make sure you also comply with any health and safety and employment regulations and any other legal responsibilities associated with your company and its industry.

If you get these issues addressed, a stress-free exit will be much easier to achieve. Remember, at this point it's not about you, it's about preparing your company for sale. Admittedly, this approach will be difficult to swallow because some of it is not something you deem important at this juncture of your company's history. But if you keep the prize in mind, the transitional process becomes easier to understand and implement. In essence, don't take your foot off the pedal; keep focused and look to grow your business in these intervening years; it will increase the bottom line and give you the freedom you need to take the next step.

Understanding Your Company

As part of the planning process, there is merit in making sure you understand the drivers of your business. This may seem idiotic since there is no doubt you know your company inside and out. But for many business owners, the longer you are at the helm the more disassociated you likely have become from your company.

Be honest; for some of you the day-to-day process is something you don't deal with any longer. Maybe it's the accounts receivable and accounts payable. You have staffers who deal with these areas of the company. Maybe you have someone in-house or an outside consultant who manages the marketing and business development aspects of your business. As for the management of your employees, your Human Resources manager makes sure everything goes well. You deal with the important stuff. Maybe you attend the weekly management meetings and the periodic project meetings. You meet with the accountant and the attorney. Perhaps you sit on a few philanthropic boards and make donations to civic projects. You're the strategic planner; the big picture person. You see it all before anyone else. Sound familiar?

Admittedly, the functions you have evolved to cover are certainly important, but they are not akin to understanding the basic nuances of your business and how it may have changed over time. Over time many of your responsibilities have changed, perhaps for a reason. Could it be you are not the manager you once were, or your attention to detail has waned as you have grown older and have become less patient? Maybe you simply are not at the office as much as you used to be. Whatever the reason, before you even begin to think of selling your company, it's worth taking stock in how your business has evolved and how it functions when you are off doing what it is you do. The best owners are those who know their company, its products, and the market inside out — and this knowledge will help you sell your business.

You'll need to be able to sum up your company's strengths and weaknesses off the top of your head. If this sounds like pretty basic research, it is, but you'd be surprised how many business owners never do the homework needed to truly view the bigger picture of their company and industry. Even if you did this work prior to launching your company or when newly formed, it's something that should be done on an ongoing basis as the industry, sector, and competitors change. It is certainly something that should be done as you prepare for sale.

Before you can begin negotiating a sale, you have to convince someone somewhere to buy your company. In this regard, the first impression is important. By reacquainting yourself with your company, you will be better prepared to tout all that is good with your company. Think carefully about your company's strengths. What makes it special? What makes it a good prospect over and above other investment opportunities? It could be your unique product, the durability of your sales, percentage of repeat customers, or the wide range and breadth of your income stream. Dig into the figures if you need to; it is only when you understand and appreciate the company in this much detail that you can sell it effectively.

Perhaps the easiest way to understand the unique needs and benefits of your company and to analyze the business is to do an updated SWOT analysis, looking at the Strengths, Weaknesses, Opportunities, and Threats inherent within your business.

The more strengths you recognize, the more opportunities the business has to grow. The weaknesses you find are immediate threats that you will want to tackle before you begin to look for a buyer for your business.

Examples of strengths can include your current financial position, the skilled workforce and latest technology you have, the beneficial transport links, and/or the strength of the company name. Is it recognized on a national, regional, or local level, for instance?

As for weaknesses, the opposite factors also hold true. If you have large debts, if your production is inefficient, if you are renting your facility and therefore paying extra costs and/or you have too much waste, for instance, these are all weaknesses you must analyze. Because this is an internal document for your eyes only, be honest and don't leave anything out. You want to identify these weaknesses in order to minimize them in the future. If you recognize that you have an unskilled workforce, for instance, you have the timeline available as part of the planning process to put a training scheme in place.

On the back of your strengths, you can assess your opportunities. Opportunities are products, ancillary markets, services, growth initiatives, mergers/acquisitions, or the introduction of technology that help make your company more profitable and attractive. The notion is that these opportunities are available for you and your company to exploit. Being in a healthy financial position, for instance, can mean the company will be in good stead for a future bank loan to expand, if needed; likewise, having already invested in new technology for your industry may mean that you could expand production at a moment's notice if the industry picks up or you decide to ramp up your output. These are great selling points to future buyers.

Likewise, on the back of your weaknesses, you can assess your threats. These may be very clear once you have summarized your weaknesses. For instance, you may have strong competition in the market, a future rise in interest rates may see the company struggle to pay back its loans, or there may be a danger that the rent for your premises is going to rise. These are all things that you will want to attempt to tackle before any future sale if you want to gain the most from your sale financially.

A SWOT analysis should help you to understand the unique constraints, growth potential, and extraneous concerns your company faces. This will help you create your management strategy for the future, aimed specifically at taking your company forward and getting it ready to sell.

How Do You Make Money?

The most important thing you understand about your business is how you make money. Let's face it, at the end of the day that's what business is all about. As rewarding as building a company from the ground up may be and as satisfying as it can be to know that you employ, train, and motivate your employees, it's all for nothing if the company doesn't make money.

You should already know how your company makes money and where it comes from; that's a crucial part of your business, and I expect you think you have this issue under control. The truth is many companies really don't make the money they have the capacity to make. You see, profits mask efficiency. The more you make, the more likely you are to throw a blind eye to how you make it. Business metrics are vitally important to a business owner, especially for those of you who really don't get involved in much of the day-to-day tasks of operating the business.

If you do not employ a business consultant, or if your accountant only provides traditional services (i.e., month-end accounting, tax filings), then I suggest you consider adding the expertise to your company. These types of professionals understand how metrics work and how they must be used if you are to push your business to greater heights. Business metrics help owners understand where the operational pitfalls exist. They give you the insight needed to know where problems are holding your company back. The competitive environment we find ourselves in today requires business owners to make timely, informed decisions. Your gut feeling may have worked in the early days but not anymore.

Remember, many buyers are looking for companies with increasing profits and growth potential, and you want to show that your profits are growing year over year with room for further fiscal development and progression.

Take the time as part of the planning process to look again at where you make your money. As you work your way towards your selling date, the insights you gain through the planning process will be of great assistance to you.

Mirror on the Wall

This section of *The Exit Equation* is for calibration purposes only. It is so vitally important that you understand why you want to leave your company and what you intend to do once you depart that we need to routinely revisit the idea.

If you think back to the earlier chapters, much was presented and discussed about the exit process and its effect on the business owner. Most important, however, was the idea that the exit planning process must start with the end in mind. That is to say, if you are going to exit your company with your money and on your terms, we need to fully understand why we want to leave and what we intend to do when we have achieved escape velocity.

Before you even begin to plan your exit strategy, you're going to have to ask yourself some questions about your future. Forget the company for a moment and look to your own personal goals. Your future and retirement are most likely why you set up the business in the first place, to bring you the sort of financial returns that enable you to live the life you want to live. You may want to sell early and leave the company before you are 55 or 60, taking advantage of the cash while you're still young enough to travel, spend more time with the family, or even get involved in new business ventures.

Or, like many other Baby Boomers, you may have originally planned early retirement only to find that you take personal satisfaction from the business world and want to involve yourself in business or some sort of organization beyond conventional retirement age. Whichever option you choose will influence how you want to leave your company and why.

Many baby boomer-aged business owners might miss the crucial point here; your business wasn't meant to be the be all and end all. It was always intended to be the means to an end. Now you just need to work out what form the next part of your life will take. It's pointless negotiating the sale of your company, for instance, if you don't know what you want out of the sale or how you want to leave. This is perhaps the fundamental point of this book: understand what you want and why.

I see too many business owners who are simply held hostage by their companies. They are tired of the rat-race but cannot seem to take the time to implement a better management process. They are frustrated with the lack of profitability but won't take the time to understand the corporate inefficiencies they allow to continue. They spend countless dollars investing in technology and equipment that promises a payback, yet they accept the fact they will never see it. They want to get out but won't put the work into the process to get what they want.

The plans you originally had when embarking on your business may no longer be relevant, so take the time now to dwell on the direction you want your life to go once you transfer your business. Consider what you personally wish to do after your current role in the company comes to an end. Will you want to continue working in some way; would you want a different job with the new owner (I wouldn't recommend it); or would members of your family want to continue working with them? What age would you want to leave and what will you do after you sell the business?

All of these things answer the "why do you want to leave" question, but they will also impact exactly *how* you will want to leave as well.

Building the Yellow Brick Road

Leaving aside *The Wonderful Wizard of Oz* as an allegory on political, economic, and social events in 1890s America, we could draw a parallel between Dorothy's trip down the Yellow Brick Road in search of the Wonderful Wizard and the Emerald City — she longed to know what was "over the rainbow" — and your own search for the perfect retirement.

Just like Dorothy, you have a journey to go on now too. The difference is that you're building the road to your future as you go along. Each and every step you take to identify your dreams, goals, and financial ambitions helps to lay another brick on that all-important Yellow Brick Road. Likewise, every task you give yourself now to boost the image of your company or to make your business all the more attractive to potential acquirers adds another brick along the path.

Every functional exit strategy is rooted in the planning process. Why you want to leave, when you want to leave, and what you want to take with you are quintessential planning issues you must acknowledge. By developing a plan and sticking to it, all future decisions as to what to buy, who to hire, what markets to go into and which you should leave are made with an end game in mind. In so doing, the realities of exiting your business on your terms can be achieved.

A Buddhist interpretation of the Yellow Brick Road is that it represents the path to self-actualization, and that's a pretty good way to look at it. You too are searching for self-fulfillment; you are looking to live the next phase of your life now and to do so as well as you can.

Your exit strategy will become your own call to adventure. And while it may be slightly more subtle than Dorothy's, you'll need the same companions as Dorothy had to see you through—*courage* (shown by the Cowardly Lion), *brains* (Scarecrow), and *heart* (the Tin Man).

Don't Cook the Books

As a business owner, you're used to giving prospective customers and clients the hard sell. Your success as a business hinges on you convincing suppliers, customers, and employees alike to work for you or with you or to buy from you on terms favorable to yourself. To reach those terms, you may have to take a little bit of artistic license or present the positives and play down the negatives.

When it comes to selling your business, however, you need to check such aggressiveness at the door. You want to be open with potential buyers and certainly so with any professional broker you may use. If you've done your own due diligence on your business in the run up to the sale, there hopefully won't be too many problems with the business; but if there are some issues, don't hide them.

Certainly, at the very least, you need to present accurate financial information; don't conceal something because you think it makes the business look bad. Buyers are aware there is no such thing as the perfect business and are likely to be much more willing to deal with any problems associated with your business during the initial decision-making process than they are if they come to light once they have decided to buy.

Sleeping dogs don't tend to lie for long; if you deliberately conceal something and get found out, the fall out could torpedo your sale. It takes a very brave buyer to stick around after you've proven you can't be trusted. It's not just the sale that you could lose either. Hiding a problem that adversely affects your business can lead to litigation.

If you do have threats or weaknesses that you can't solve at the time of selling, be honest about them and try to suggest a solution. It may be that a small cash injection by the buyer, something you're not currently in a position to do (or want to do) could solve the problem. Make an effort to identify potential solutions to make sure the sale is still attractive in the buyer's eyes. Having some problems with the business doesn't necessarily mean it won't command an attractive price.

Buyers want to know you are selling in good faith; if they find you lied or misrepresented even a small important fact, they are going to wonder what else you're hiding and fear that taking on a business run by someone who can't be trusted will end up being a noose around their necks. Suddenly, from one sleeping dog, you seem to have a whole animal shelter's worth!

Stick to the Script—the Most Difficult Thing an Owner Must Do

Once you do all your homework, research and identify your personal goals, and create a plan of action, you'll be tempted to do one more thing—forget about them all. As life takes hold again, your company will try to suck you into its typical day of demanding more and more of your time. When this happens, it's easy to forget your script.

Yes, your succession planning needs to have some degree of flexibility to react to changes in the industry, market, or even within your company, but don't throw the baby out with the bathwater. If you want to retire or move on to something else, keep to the plan. Don't imagine you can ignore it for a couple of years and then start again; you'll either end up trapped by your own company or end up walking away without the money you need to make a difference to your life.

Use the timeframe you have established to really work your plan and see your dreams come to fruition. Take heart in the fact that you have planned your work carefully and have given yourself the time you need to examine all options and create the best exit strategy for you. Whenever you feel run down or you get caught up in the proverbial chase and begin to question everything (the time will come, trust me), put your faith in the plan. You have planned your work; now is the time to work your plan.

Just like Dorothy, if you veer away from the Yellow Brick Road, you'll regret it. Stick to the plan; stick to your own Yellow Brick Road and find your own rainbow!

The Three Most Important Things in Business & in Departing Your Company

Entrepreneurs who survive the initial start-up stage and find themselves on the cusp of being business owners quickly discover the secret to business success: cash flow. Cash is king, and without it, you simply will not survive. It does not matter how flashy your business plan is or how many business coaches you have consulted, nor does it matter how great your product/service is or the extent to which your marketing plan will help cultivate a vibrant market for your business. The simple truth is cash is your heartbeat. Everything you hope to achieve and that which is fundamental to the survival of your business can be boiled down to this one vital ingredient.

This reality is not much different on the backend of the entrepreneurial process. When it comes to preparing your company for sale, **cash flow remains the king of the land.**

A healthy cash flow statement is likely to sell the company for you; it is what the buyer wants to see. No matter how many factories or offices you have, how ambitious your company has been in the past, or how many people you employ, the simple assessment of the vitality and success of your business boils down to the same common denominator: cash flow.

Despite cash's predominance in the realm of your business valuation, there are other matters that require your attention. The second all-important factor in selling and departing your company is that of self-prophecy. There is the inevitable flaw in the fundamental notion that once your business has been prepared for sale and you are willing to let it go, buyers will quickly clamor to consummate a deal. Although we would all like to think the sale process would be easy and timely, the reality of the situation is that such opportunities are not in your control.

Many business owners have prepared themselves and their businesses for sale only to find there are few interested buyers because of factors beyond the control of the seller. As stated previously, timing is everything, but it is impossible to guarantee a sale simply because you and your company are now ready. One way to circumvent a very real timing threat is to not wait for a buyer to come to you; be proactive and **create your own buy-out scenario**. Consider how to best structure your business so it can buy you out. Granted, this is not always an easy process and a lot depends on the type of business you own, but many times, whether you would prefer a management buy-out, family succession, or a straight asset sale, business owners can structure a process so the company begins to liquidate your equity share. We will talk about this prospect a bit later in this chapter.

The third important aspect of preparing your company for sale is **attitude**. You need to be in the right mind for a sale, by which I mean you need to take from it what *you* need. It's all too easy to let emotion and a feeling of duty hamstring your succession plans; this is the company you created from the ground up; it's natural that you want to find someone who will keep the success going. Likewise, you may feel a debt of duty and responsibility to the people you hired, some of whom you no doubt lured away from rival companies with equally good jobs. So it stands to reason that you'd want to find a buyer who will protect the integrity of the company you have built and the employees who ensure its continued success. This is a noble position, but at the end of the day, the success of your post-business ownership will be gauged by your attention to detail and putting yourself ahead of everyone else.

We are going to talk about each of these three elements in turn in more detail. The most important issue first...

Cash Flow, Cash Flow, Cash Flow

If you're anything like all of the other small business owners in America, you are used to looking at your company's revenue and expenses in terms of minimizing your taxable income. That's a realistic strategy for *running* your business, but it may not be the best strategy for *selling* your business. From an exit strategy perspective, **cash flow remains the king of the land.**

A potential purchaser wants to get a feel for the real cash flow of the business and will go so far as to base their decisions on it, so you need to make sure the profit and loss accounts you present don't underestimate the cash you're bringing in from operations. Ditto the value of the investments you hold.

Also, like many other business owners, the line between your personal expenses and those of the company has become finer and finer over the years; perhaps even to a point where some expenses are indistinguishable. You see, as businesses attain a level of success and business owners become increasingly synonymous with their companies, owners tend to over-reach and use the assets of the business as though they were their own. Although you believe you have every right to decide what is right and fair, these expenses do detract from the value of your company. So, you need to make sure they are accounted for.

In addition, perhaps you made some business decisions over the past few years based on your personal needs and lifestyle. For instance, maybe you opened an office or retail site in a location close to where you like to vacation; or perhaps you have diversified your business to include equipment, services, or products that are tied to ancillary family or friend relationships. Maybe you bought a corporate vehicle for yourself, attended a trade show in an exotic location, or even paid yourself a bonus that was beyond the reasonable means of your business. These "discretionary expenses" are really profits which you chose to divert for personal interest or gain. These expenses need to be recognized for what they are, profits, and added back into your Profit/Loss Statement through recasting.

The recasting process was introduced in Chapter 3 and relates to the valuation of your company. Discretionary expenses should not be hidden, and you should not be ashamed of them. In fact, by acknowledging they exist you are giving testament to a potential buyer that your business can, and does, support a lifestyle which is over and above how the company performs on paper.

Recasting your earnings is reasonable and prudent if you want to obtain a truer value of your company during the selling process. In the end, when it comes to assessing your cash flow, there are three main types of cash flow to consider:

operational cash flow, investing cash flow, and financing cash flow. Each has benefits and drawbacks for you, the seller, and equally, attractions and limitations for the buyer.

Operating Cash Flow

In a nutshell, operating cash flow refers to the amount of cash your company generates from sales. For those more astute financial managers in the group, it is the earnings before interest and taxes, plus depreciation, less income taxes. Investors (business buyers) focus on operating cash flow because it can identify companies that are spending dollars faster than getting dollars in the door. A positive operating cash flow number indicates a healthy company, while a negative ratio shows signs of cash flow problems.

If your business has numerous fixed assets on its books—perhaps machinery or factories—you will want to take depreciation into account. As depreciation is a non-cash expense, a simple net income quote will fail to show the true picture of your company as the depreciation will lower the net income. Operational cash flow takes this issue into account.

Buyers traditionally like to see your operational cash flow because it highlights any liquidity issues a company may have and truly demonstrates the quality of a company's earnings. A simple net income or earnings quote, in contrast, can be misleading; a company can show positive net earnings and yet still not be able to pay its debts. Cash flow is vital for paying the bills!

Any negative cash flow statement must have an explanation for the negativity to keep it attractive to buyers. If your current operational cash flow shows negative, for instance, you must be able to show it was as a result of a one-time expenditure that will not be repeated, such as a new acquisition or a new factory. Any company that has a consistent negative operating cash flow will simply not be appealing to buyers.

Investment Cash Flow (aka Free Cash Flow)

The second type of cash flow that could be useful to you when selling your company is investment cash flow. This reports the collective or aggregate *change* in your company's cash position as a result of any gains or losses from investments in fixed assets. Also defined as free cash flow, this economic assessment value is defined as operating cash flow less capital expenditures less acquisitions. Obviously, capital expenditures are those expenses necessary to remain competitive in the market, such as buying new computer technology, equipment, and other capital investments. A company with a positive free cash flow is healthy for investors because after paying off all its current expenses (e.g., salaries and wages and short-term debt), the company has enough cash flow to make necessary capital investments to grow the company.

We're talking land, buildings, equipment, fixtures, vehicles, and furniture, as well as long-term investments, such as sales of subsidiaries and loans to other companies or acquisitions (or sales) of other companies. For instance, money spent on additions to property, as well as purchases or sales of securities, affects investment cash flow.

Cash coming into the company from any of the above is a positive cash flow; money leaving the company for these same reasons is a negative cash flow, even if it is a purchase of a long-term asset, as the acquisition will reduce cash in the business itself.

Adding this investment cash flow can help to even out an overall negative cash flow situation. When it can be proved that the negative cash flow is a result of heavy investment, potential purchasers of your company are much more likely to look favorably upon the value of your company.

Financing Cash Flow

Financing cash flow reports the changes in balances of cash between a company and its owners and creditors. It accounts for external activities such as issuing or selling more stock, issuing cash dividends, and adding or changing loans.

It takes into account items such as notes payable (again due after one year, also includes loans from the bank), any deferred income taxes (establishing any difference between the income tax appearing on the company's statements and actual income tax appearing on the company's tax returns) and preferred stock (allowing preferential treatment of dividends to preferred stockholders).

Other factors also considered include any bonds payable (the amount of bonds issued by the company that are outstanding), shares of common stock, retained earnings, and shareholders' equity credit balance accounts.

In short, it is the cash received from the issuing of stock or debt *minus* the amount paid as dividends and spent on the repurchasing of debt or stock.

Financing cash flow alone can have drawbacks as the standard to assess your company's value; it can impact your company's net cash flow in a way that contradicts how your company is actually performing.

A profitable company, for instance, that wants to pay down its debt or retire long-term debt can actually look less promising on paper as a result of the financing cash flow assessment; if you're unlucky, it could even render your net cash flow zero even though you have a strong operating performance.

If this is the position your company finds itself in, be prepared to explain the situation and show the evidence. In the end, it is far better to have a company that is financially strong "in paper" rather than "on paper."

Next, let's look at how you can create your own buy-out scenario…

Create Your Own Buy-Out Scenario

There is a massive gap between the desire entrepreneurs have to sell their businesses and the ability to execute a plan. By many anecdotal accounts, over 50% of most small business owners want to sell their companies, but only one percent actually accomplish the feat each year. Why? Because those who successfully sell do so by recognizing what buyers want. This is why it is fruitful to spend some time assessing the strength of your company by **creating your own buy-out scenario.**

Small business owners who successfully sell their enterprises are creating cash-flow-positive companies with self-directed management teams who understand their market and clientele and sell a scalable product or service. These business owners and their management teams understand their niche and market costs and follow their own rules as to the projects and clients they'll accept. They keep long-term operational and developmental costs down, maximize efficiency, and they stop playing games with the taxman. In short, they focus on equity and perceived value— just like the business owner did once he survived the first few years and decided to grow the company for the long-term. Somewhere along the way, as business owners skewed the line between personal and corporate interests, the direction of the company became misguided and the operational profits were used for selfish and nonperforming reasons. So in order to rebuild the business for sale, successful sellers are building companies that run well without them and transfer ownership easily.

The successful seller will be one who creates his own selling opportunities, and no matter what type of company you have, that's a possibility open to all. You just need to recognize your options, evaluate which makes the most sense for you and your business and then get out there and make it happen!

Let's take a look at the options you potentially have for selling your business:

Management Buy-Out

A management buy-out may well be the best scenario for you and your business; if you play it right, it could offer you the cash you need without the hassle of searching for a new buyer for your company.

Your managers already have experience running the company; they have an understanding of the company's value; and crucially, will most likely have the motivation to become their own boss.

They could be the best chance for you to escape the business with whatever you need to free you and to know your company and employees will—presumably—be in good hands (you hired and trained them after all!).

When you consider your time horizon and your personal needs, consider *who* on your staff you would like to sell to. Identify the key managers or members of staff that you think will have the ambition and potential to own and operate their own business. Broach the subject hesitantly because you do not want to create an uneasy feeling between your key managers and the general rank and file staffers. The subject and its discussions must be handled discreetly, always giving yourself an out if the key managers you are talking to do not have an interest or the idea could likely create a rift between select members of your management team. Even more importantly, be cognizant that not all your key managers likely run in the same circles or have the same expectations when it comes to the company. In many instances, the only common interest these folks have is their employer, so talk about who might want to purchase the company may leave some managers wondering how they would fit in if another member they do not particularly care for became their boss. If you do decide to bring the issue up in conversation, do more listening than talking.

If you opt for a management buy-out and your top tier of managers are on board, you can probably expedite the time horizon because of the familiarity each of the parties has with the company and each other.

It is important to establish an exact date for when the changeover will happen. Don't just say "when I'm too tired to run the company" or "sometime after I turn 60"; it's all too easy to get carried along by the wave of daily chores or the satisfaction of a job well done and to "forget" that you meant to step down. Your managers won't be willing to wait forever, so don't put them through it; pick a changeover date and stick to it.

What's more, you should *work* towards it as well. Now is the time to train those members of your staff on all the roles and responsibilities you currently shoulder as owner. Teach them about the business and about marketing; promote them to positions of more responsibility where possible, and generally, mentor them about the running of the business day to day.

There is an argument that in these instances you may want to stay on as a part-time consultant for the first few months following the transfer to give your managers and new owners a helping hand where needed. Although admirable and beneficial to you in the form of an easily earned supplemental income, the reality is it is better to walk out the front door on the day the sale is consummated. It is inevitable that the new owners, even though they may have served you admirably and went along with all your plans and tactics, may not want to run the company the same way you did. Do not stay on if you are likely to struggle with the transition; if you cannot accept that new blood and ideas may be beneficial to the company, don't torture yourself by having to watch it.

This issue will be covered in further detail later in the book.

Selling to Family

Another potential option open to you is to sell to family. If you are considering family succession, it's important that you ask yourself a few key questions—both for your sake and theirs. You don't want to force succession on someone, for instance, or make them feel obliged to carry on the family business if that's not what they really want to do. If they don't have their heart in it, the business and morale will suffer.

So, before you broach a family succession plan, consider if your intended successor really wants to take over, if they have the right skills, and if it could cause conflict within the business or with other family members if you announce that you are doing so. Don't forget to put yourself first as well; don't opt for a family succession if it's not really the best option to free your cash. Don't fall for the lure of passing the business on to someone with the same family name.

While you may want to pass on the company to your first-, second-, or third-born, or even someone else in the family, ask yourself: will it really work for you? Will it sufficiently provide you what you need for *your* future; will it be tax efficient? Ask yourself the hard questions and consider — would someone else in the business who isn't family actually be a better bet? Would they be more likely to take the business forward or to give you the return you need to free yourself from the company shackles? All options should be on the table at this stage.

If you do decide to turn the business over to a family member, how should you go about it? How do you create a family-led exit strategy that eases the way for you to enter retirement?

First, I'd recommend you opt for just one successor from the family if you can, assuming it is practical and realistic. When choosing the successor, take into account the potential threat of future conflict (you want your choice to have the support of your workforce) and consider objectively who can best take the business forward.

Secondly, don't feel obliged to share the succession equally with all of your offspring if your instincts tell you they are not right for the role. You must act impartially now to safeguard the future of the company and the employees who place their trust in you, after you have looked after yourself, of course.

Besides, you can always be financially fair to your other children in other ways, such as taking out a life insurance policy for their benefit or giving non-voting right shares to your company. They do not have to be involved in the future management of the business if you think they will not add anything of value.

Thirdly, if you do choose more than one successor, protect the company by ensuring they each have a separate area of responsibility and there are formal dispute procedures in place. Appointing an independent Board of Directors can also protect the company in times of disagreement.

And finally, when going ahead with family succession, you can make your exit smoother by establishing a few things ahead of time. The most important thing you will need to determine is if you want, or will have, any future role in the business; likewise, you must accept that if you sell the business or pass it on to family, you will not be in charge anymore. Just like the management buy-out option, you will have to accept that the new boss may have very different ideas from your own.

You may need extra strong willpower here to force yourself to avoid "butting" in; your advice and support may be invaluable to your family, but just because the new owner is your son doesn't mean he has to listen to or obey you. Neither does it mean you have the right to criticize his management techniques.

You need to find a way to distance yourself from the company's operations to make it easier on everyone, yourself and the new owner included. This may be easier to manage if you agree to a deal whereby you are no longer financially dependent on the company's success once you hand over the keys.

In a manner just like you would with a management buy-out, give your successor all the preparation you can ahead of time by training them, promoting them, and perhaps encouraging them to work in each section of the business to get an understanding of your company from the ground up.

Don't just decide to go for a family succession and then parachute your loved one into position; just because he or she may be a chip off the old block doesn't mean they instinctively know how to run your business. Genes aren't that powerful! Giving them the time to truly learn the business — again, another reason why your time horizon is so important — will help them manage the process and hopefully give them the opportunity to earn the respect of your employees at the same time.

Selling to Another Company

Management buy-outs and family succession aside, the most common way of selling your business is usually by selling to another business, often one already involved in the same industry.

You will need to decide if you want to sell all or just part of the business. You could sell a portion of your shares to raise the money needed for retirement, for instance, or you could sell select assets and then liquidate the remainder that the buyer does not want.

Whatever option you decide, you must look into the tax implications (of selling company shares versus selling the business itself/company assets). This is an extremely important consideration. How the deal is structured and what is sold must be considered so you can limit your tax obligations. It is commonplace for a business owner to be fixated on the sales price and then once the accountant completes your tax return, that large nest egg you thought you had is shrunk considerably after Uncle Sam takes his fair share. In short, you cannot do this in a vacuum. When it is all said and done, the terms of the deal are far more important than the price. More of this later in the book.

Self-Financing the Sale

As you're looking for potential buyers for your company, you may come across one key issue—the desire is there to buy your promising business, but the money isn't. A shortage of business deal financing is preventing many deals from getting off the ground, but there is something you can do about that, *if* you want to.

You can self-finance the deal. Namely, consider financing at least part of the sale in order to get the deal done. Self-financing business deals have long been a positive for many buyers, but in today's cash-strapped market, it's even more of a selling point. It may be the only way that you can get your sale done. At the very least, being open to the idea will give you a lot more options.

By offering financing, you, the business seller, would allow the buyer to make a down payment with the remainder being paid over time. Although the notion of selling and carrying the note is not an option for some, in a market which rewards initiative, seller financing may be the key to a deal.

Before you even consider this option, however, you should be aware that it does come with some risks. If you want a complete severing of ties with the business in order to move on, this option certainly doesn't allow for that. By offering seller financing, you are still tied to the business AND reliant on the business continuing to turn a profit so the new owner can make required payments to you.

That may go well if the business is still a good going concern under the new owner's guidance, but if it starts to struggle, you could face the concept of losing the interest income and experiencing extra costs as part of dealing with the collection of debt. You must be confident of the prospective owner and the company's ability to generate profits in the future. You will also want to ensure you take enough cash up front to mitigate the risk.

You may want to waive some of this, of course, if you are selling to a family member, but again, be aware of the risk involved and make sure you're thinking rationally and not emotionally. If you have any doubts or concerns or even a bad gut feeling, don't do it, no matter how much you may want to sell or how much pressure a potential buyer may put on you. It's no small risk so make sure both your head and your heart — and your guts — support the idea.

Of course, self-financing can actually bring you advantages if done correctly. In these situations, the asking price is usually somewhat inflated as a means of the risk-taking. Likewise, most sales using seller financing can bring a higher than market interest rate over the life of the loan.

Liquidation

Finally, if all else fails and you want to dissolve your company, you could opt for voluntary liquidation. Liquidation is usually a last ditch attempt to get as much money out of a company as possible before you shut it down and walk away.

In this case, all the company's assets will be converted to cash to pay creditors, outstanding wages, administrator costs and other required payments. Liquidation is traditionally entered into by companies struggling with debt, meaning the owner can walk away without debt hanging over his or her head, but it can also be done by solvent companies wishing to voluntarily wind up the business and dissolve.

Assets, machinery, equipment and real estate belonging to the company are all liquidated and the cash redistributed. You'd certainly be free then.

As always, choose the best option for you and no one else.

Sell With the Right Attitude

When it comes to selling the business you lovingly nurtured and grew over the past decades, it can be difficult to be hard-hearted about it. You may want to judge the sale in terms of how well the new owner would look after your staff or how confident you are that the new owner will keep your legacy and grow the company.

Don't get me wrong; these are legitimate concerns, BUT you shouldn't be putting them ahead of your own need to take as much money out of the company as you can. You are selling in order to finance the next phase of your life and maybe even your family's life; don't ever forget that. That one fact alone has to be *the* most important element of the sale. You come first; everyone else is a distant runner-up.

There is no loyalty when it comes to selling your business; don't be concerned about loyalty to your staffers. In fact, I'd even advise you not to tell them that you want to sell until the deal is done (unless you'd prefer a management buy-out, of course). Confidentiality is the key in selling negotiations.

No matter how much you may trust your key employees or managers, keep your lips pursed. Remember, you don't owe them anything, so don't feel obliged to tell them you want to sell. Confiding in the wrong person can undo all the good work you've done over the years before you even get around to selling. A careless word from someone in the know, a change in attitude, or even gossip can snowball and cause all sorts of trouble for your company.

Nothing unsettles a workforce more than news that the business may be sold. Some will believe the company is in trouble, even if that is not the case, while others will fear what could happen to their jobs if another owner takes control. Your workforce is the biggest asset you have—and something a potential buyer will most likely want to retain. It's a big selling point and the last thing you need is for your employees to abandon ship at the mere suggestion of a business sale.

At some point, a potential buyer will come along, and you will be flattered. In light of all those years of stress and anxiety, the distant sale of your business you thought might never happen seems to present itself at light speed. Your initial reluctance as to the potential of the deal because it seems too good to be true eventually turns to giddiness. This surreal turn of events rekindles the spark in your eye. Your thoughts turn from making payroll and dealing with employee healthcare to sunshine and relaxation. Could this be true; can all of the turmoil and surmounting burdens of business ownership actually be over? How is it this is really happening?

Your giddiness will turn to eagerness. Now you WANT to leave; you are ready. The opportunity to be free again is chilling. You begin to daydream of all the things you have wanted to do but simply could never find the time or energy to do them. "Holy cow, I'm going to sell my business!" is now your constant thought. You are quick to forget the apprehensiveness you felt when your thoughts first centered on exiting your company. Although once you felt you could never do it, didn't want to do it, couldn't afford it, and you were not sure what else you would do if you left, now your thoughts are solely leveraged on the idea of leaving. Your eagerness to consummate the deal morphs to self-imposed pressure to sell. After all the challenges to survive, let alone succeed as a business owner, you understand the clarity of the issue; this is a great opportunity.

The buyer, for reasons you do not know and quite frankly are not concerned with, wants to get the deal done quickly. Negotiations go smoothly and quickly. You smirk at the thought of selling your business and challenges portrayed by business consultants like me who warned you of the intent, process, and timing of selling your business. The tripping hazards have been minimal and the naysayers be damned. You think, "There is no way I am going to look back on this with regret." Life is good, and it is about the get much better.

At some point, this little make-believe scenario might come true for you. For many business owners, the epiphany of the benefits of selling their business only comes into focus when the deal is real. But remember—selling without selling out starts before you sit at the negotiating table. For all the reasons you know why you want and need to sell your business, there is much to be said for knowing how to sell. Understanding the company's valuation, setting a sales price floor, and gauging the buyer's ceiling price are necessary to create the negotiating parameters. And perhaps most importantly, business owners must be prepared for the buyer to lower his offer at the last minute after you have committed emotionally to selling. It happens all the time.

Letting go of a deal can be tough for entrepreneurial business owners who are, by their nature, innately competitive. It is for these reasons *The Exit Equation* has you begin with the end in mind. When you put things in perspective and remember why you want to sell your equity and what you need in return, the ensuing battle between your heart and your head that comes from negotiations gone bad can be put in check. When you start with the end in mind and remain committed to a plan that is designed around you and your aspirations and desires for the final third of your life, the emotional and logical push-and-pull of negotiations do not need to lead to regret.

When it comes to what you think your company is worth and what you want from a sale, do not compromise; in a compromise, someone loses. You don't want that to be you. Instead, seek a consensus — in a consensus, everyone wins!

Remember, you don't want what's right, you want what's yours.

The Cost of Doing Business and Impact on the Deal

Last year I had the pleasure of working with a small business owner named Tom, who operated a successful light manufacturing business. He had grown up in the business. It was started by his grandfather and was eventually operated by his father. Soon, he had controlling interest of the business, but after years of struggles, the business was being prepared for sale. It was sad, but expected. No one in the family really wanted to be part of the operation any longer, and given his age, it was time for Tom to move on to the next phase of his life. The challenges of selling the business were not a surprise, as the business and the family had never gone through the sales process before.

One of the critical issues in preparation of the sale of the business was that of its cost of doing business. This may seem shocking, but too many times business owners really do not understand the valuation drivers of the business. Yes, they buy supplies and materials, they pay craftsmen to manufacture the product, and the product is marketed and sold. It seems simple enough, and it shouldn't be difficult for a business owner to cite the company's valuation drivers. Tom, like many of his peers, did not have a good handle on how the corporate money was being spent, what the market conditions were for his product, what the status of his competitors were, and how his technology played into his competitive market advantage. He was so busy working in the business to try to make ends meet that he had taken his eye off the prize and failed to work on the business. As we worked through the process of preparing him and his business for sale, many of the issues that were once thought to be disadvantages were not that at all. To say Tom was surprised is a huge understatement.

When it comes to selling your business, you need to know the *cost* of doing business in order to establish a reasonable expectation of value.

Knowing your company inside and out and really taking the time to understand how it makes money, how it spends money and where it stands in the market are the key valuation drivers of your business. The more you understand what factors contribute to the value of your business, the better you can formulate a successful exit strategy and ultimately put more money in your pocket.

If you are like many other business owners, Tom included, your gut instinct has served you well over the years. In reality however, the longer you are in business the more your gut instinct works to your disadvantage. Where anecdotal information allows you to be nimble and quick when your business is young, the lack of metrics hurts your business immeasurably as the business matures. This transition is not surprising when you consider how much of your time is redirected to activities and issues that are not important to the financial performance of your company. At some point, the time comes to make amends for not keeping your eye on the important issues affecting your business and for not starting your business with the end in mind. As you begin to run out of the ambition necessary to move your company forward, your gut instinct is no longer valuable when it comes to preparing your company for sale. You need to base your exit strategy on cold hard facts.

Knowing Your Company

At first blush, this section of the book may seem petty. If you thought the same, shame on you. I bet when you were younger you knew your business very well. You were involved in every detail and intrinsically knew where your company stood at any point in time. Your business was an extension of you—**you needed the business**. Over time business owners tend to tip the scale in the opposite direction—making **the business need you**. This is a challenge when you start to formulate an exit strategy.

What does your company do? What has got you here so far? How do you make money?

It may sound like we are getting back to basics, and you're right; we are. But you'd be surprised just how many business owners launch their companies in a blaze of glory, manage it to a level of success, and then try to sell without ever really looking at the fundamental drivers of the business.

The majority of American companies are in the professional, scientific, and technical services sectors according to the five-year 2007 Survey of Business Owners (accounting for 14% of U.S. companies). Construction represents 12.6% of companies, while the one-time mainstays of American business, manufacturing and agriculture, now only account for 2.3% and 1% respectively.

Every single one of these companies, no matter what the size or sector, has unique issues, achievements, concerns, revenues, and expenditures; some of these will be dictated by the sector, others by the company itself, and still others by the sort of owner or managers they have in place. Why am I telling you this? Well, it's simple. I am telling you this because you need to know exactly what your company's unique considerations are and why.

Traditionally, "How will I make money?" was one of the important questions you needed to answer before you started your business; you needed to include the information in a business plan if you wanted a loan from the bank to get your business off the ground. Nowadays, however, since the advent of the Internet, which continues to reduce barriers to entry, many companies launch without any idea of how they will make money.

Even those like you, who launched your business years ago and would no doubt have analyzed the potential income issue ahead of time, may have forgotten to revisit the topic once the company was up and running. As the owner of the company, you were sure you knew what made it tick, what attracted customers, and exactly what they were willing to pay for; your company was your baby—of course you knew! You could tell anybody off the top of your head just where the money came from at any given time.

That is, of course, impressive if true, BUT a lot of business owners have been shocked to discover their instincts weren't always right. Companies change over time. Technological advances can change the face of the industry overnight, new competitors can alter a level playing field, social media can be a friend or foe, and the Internet can play havoc with your established lines of distribution.

Unless you can say truthfully that you have kept up with all of these and more, it might be time to set aside your instinct-based management style and look for cold, hard facts instead.

Understanding Your Competitive Advantage

While you're ascertaining exactly where your money is coming from, you might also want to take the time to objectively review your company's competitive advantage as well.

When you consider the answer to the simple question — why *should* customers still buy from you rather than from a competitor? — there are usually two fundamental answers: either your product or service is cheaper than your competitors, or it is differentiated from your competitors. Namely, people can't buy the exact same product anywhere else.

As a small business, you may have been able to offer a lower-priced product thanks to reduced overhead costs, though this often becomes difficult to maintain if you want to grow the business (when overhead costs inevitably rise). On the flip side, if you can differentiate your product or service it may appeal to a specific target market because of perceived benefits in serviceability, value, performance, or attractiveness. The type of product or service you offer and your competitive advantage will influence the perception of your company in the eyes of a potential purchaser, the amount of money you make, the future potential of your company and its corporate value, and the price you can ask at sale. Understanding the nuances of these elements will guide you in how far you can push your sale and how much leverage you have with the price.

When the time comes to discuss your business with a potential buyer, don't just rattle off anecdotal "facts"; your gut instinct isn't good enough in this scenario. If you are dealing with a sophisticated buyer, any discrepancy between your recitation of the "facts" and those uncovered during the due diligence process is sure to haunt you as negotiations unfold. Your competitive advantage can come in many forms and are, sometimes, easily disguised. For instance, if your computer information technology system, inclusive of its software, is up-to-date and all licenses are in place, this can be a huge advantage to companies who rely on managing large quantities of data. If your licenses are not up-to-date, this could pose a large expense to a buyer after the sale. Likewise, if you own specific patents or trademarks, especially those that do not expire anytime soon, your company has greater value. Also, maybe you control a large client account, one that all your competitors wish they had but don't. Presuming you have a way of securing that account for a reasonable period of time despite your departure from the company, a potential buyer will likely sit up and take notice.

Competitive advantages can also be discreet but effective nonetheless: employing a key technical person; having a relationship with a regulator, bureaucrat, or politician; or owning the rights to the biggest brand in town are all advantages that prospective buyers are interested in. These are just a few of the valuation drivers for your business and assets you need to understand and tout as negotiations unfold.

Now the bad news; there are also competitive disadvantages you need to either fix or hide. Perhaps too much business is concentrated in too few customers. Having all (or most) of your eggs in one basket is, for most businesses, business suicide. Maybe your building lease is near the end of its term. This could lead to an uptick in rent over the long term. Then, of course, there is the rising star scenario. his occurs when you have a staffer who controls a large segment of your business and they are beginning to realize their leverage and the power that comes with it. These are but a few sprinkles of the competitive disadvantages your company bears, and these could lead to a lower cost proposal from a potential buyer. I strongly suggest you take notice of the issues within your company that have gotten away from you. These are the issues that either cost you money (in terms of excess expenses and staff inefficiencies) or are holding back your company in terms of its overall performance. Continue to look for ways to innovate throughout your company; match your business needs and its operations to your technological abilities (e.g., your computer IT system should never be maintained in either an under- or over-capacity situation); and ensure you have the right people on the right job for the right reason.

And in the end, don't forget to consider where you've come from and the glide path your company is currently on; there is something to be said for sustainability.

Where Do You Spend Your Money?

As well as looking at your income streams and how you make money, you're also going to want to take an impartial—and fact-led—eye to your cash outlays as well. Namely, where does your company spend its money?

Again, being forewarned is forearmed. Looking at this topic ahead of time not only helps you to better understand the cash appetite of your company—the real company, not the

David Saint-Onge

one you have in your head — but also allows you to fix the cash sinkholes that afflict every company.

The simple fact is the longer a company is in business, the greater the cost creep. Over time, everything costs more — from little things like trash disposal, office supplies, and utilities — to major expenditures, including salaries, fringe benefits, corporate insurance, and marketing.

In addition to the obvious are the business relationships you keep and what those relationships cost you to operate. For instance, if you own a consulting practice and in service to your clients, you use the services of a few sub-consultants like a website designer or marketing agency, are you leveraging those relationships and the fact you are engaging these services in a non-competitive environment in exchange for a cost reduction? If not, shame on you. Maybe you are in the construction business and your trusty subs are not providing you reasonable discounts for providing them a steady stream of business and timely payments. In these scenarios and many more just like them, businesses incur ever increasing costs by not leveraging their buying power. Creating a valuable business and readying it for sale means addressing the cash sinkholes you have grown to accept.

On the flip side of the obscure are the obvious. Your business also spends its money on assets, materials, labor, and operating costs. You may also have spent money on financing an expansion in order to boost production capacity — spending on new technology, such as tools, machinery, and computer systems — or investing money to develop new products or to enter new markets.

Small businesses in the United States were forecast to spend $125 billion on advanced technology in 2011. Did you join them? This spending could have taken many guises; companies just like yours were predicted to spend 29% of their lead generation budget on blogs and social media (Source: International Data Corporation).

These are costs that detract from short-term profits and, on appearance, tend to devalue your company. Make sure you total these discretionary expenses so a buyer can better understand the profit margin of your company.

Protecting Your Sacred Cows

While we're at it, let's consider your sacred cows. By that I mean what special purchases, charities, or interests do you have and how does your loyalty to these causes affect the financial position of your company?

You see, business owners are warm blooded. They tend to give of themselves and, in turn, their companies, to help those who need it. These are your sacred cows — the causes you feel strongly about and willingly spend your company resources on because they are important to you, not necessarily your company.

Maybe you sponsor a series of youth sports team; perhaps you give generously to United Way. Of course, there is always the local hospital charity, sponsorship of major golf tournaments, or perhaps Habitat for Humanity. Regardless of your interest, these ventures consume cash, labor, or other disposable company resources that detract from the financial viability of your company. Certainly, you will argue the intrinsic benefits outweigh the costs, but when selling your company, these special endeavors need to be accounted for so their true value can be factored into the value of your company.

As I have said before, at some point the pendulum swings from the owner serving the business, to the business serving the owner. It is inevitable—almost everyone does it to some degree. It is certainly your prerogative to make these choices, but you should endeavor to ensure you are getting credit for it.

Sacrificial Lambs

Everyone has a walk-away price or a walk-away condition. Have you given any thought to what yours might be?

It is the basis of negotiation, but it's often something business owners often neglect. Why? Because the euphoria that comes from sitting across the table from someone who is willing to buy your company and the prospect that the transaction will inflate your bank account balance is compelling. And when compelled to do something that seems like finding the pot of gold at the end of the rainbow, the inevitable euphoria generally leads to poor decisions and compromise. When this happens, the unconditional issues of the sale you once held dear are now quickly compromised because you want so badly to do the deal. These issues are your sacrificial lambs.

Let's start with the sales price. In a buyer's market, the prospective purchaser will have a slew of ammunition to argue why your company should sell near, at, or below the floor of your sales range. Unstable equity markets, difficulty in obtaining capital, the potential for inflation, and the advent of universal healthcare are all unknowns and with unknowns comes value depreciation. You must have a minimum sales price for your sale; anything less than your minimum and you need to have the courage to just walk away. Even though this will be hard to do, it is imperative. In tight economic markets, savvy businessmen look for the deals where they can spend dimes on a dollar to acquire the next great bargain. Accept the fact that this tactic is a reality. If you build and maintain a solid company that brings value, you will get more courters, but some of them will be less than honorable.

With regard to payment of the purchase price, you might be asked to carry some of the paper. Such a request is certainly not unusual, especially if the buyer is willing to pay a premium sales price and that premium cannot be financed through traditional means. There is a strong urge here to take the premium payment and accept the risk, but keep in mind these are land contracts and the risks can be steep. Are you prepared to come back into the company and repair the damage caused by someone who promised the moon but failed to deliver? In such an instance your company's reputation, let alone its financial solvency, the attitude of the staff, and the willingness of your customers to hang with you might be irreparable. Many business owners are lured into these arrangements because the purchase price is so damn good, but when a significant portion is deferred, look out. In some circumstances, these types of corporate purchases work just fine, but understand the ramifications if it fails.

Another important consideration when it comes to sacrificial lambs is that of a covenant not-to-compete. These concessions may seem minuscule, but they have lasting effects. There is plenty of debate in the business and legal professions as to the validity and enforceability of these agreements. By most accounts, to be reasonably enforceable, such an agreement must not be unduly burdensome to the departing employee/owner and needs to accommodate the following parameters:

1. It must protect a legitimate business interest. An enforceable covenant not-to-compete cannot encompass presumed future services and should be limited to the current services of the company;
2. The timeline should not be excessive. My experience suggests timeframes of less than five years are likely to be considered reasonable by any judicial body who may be asked to enforce such an agreement;
3. The geographic area of the restriction must also be considered. To include regions of the country in which the company does not already compete appears to be extreme and may prove impeachable; and,
4. There must be specific financial compensation to make the agreement stand up. In the instance of a business sale, some portion of the sales price must be identified as compensation to the soon-to-be former business owner; the overall deal itself simply does not work. Another consideration is that such compensation is taxed differently by Uncle Sam than are the proceeds of the business sale; so make sure you consult your tax advisor when contemplating such an arrangement.

Another sacrifice asked of you may be for you to stay on as a consultant for a period of time. In some instances the buyer may ask that a portion of the sales price be provided in the form of an employment agreement or some portion of the sales price is directly tied to the company's performance during a specific "transition timeframe." In many instances, these types of requests are conditions of a premium sales price. If you consider these arrangements, recognize a few important issues likely to surface. The first relates to your continued service to the company as a consultant. Remember, in such a role your opinion means nothing. The new owner might consider your thoughts and might not. Their management style inevitably will not be similar to your style. These are obvious signs of future friction and given the fact you were the boss one day and the company was yours to direct, taking a backseat to someone else will be extremely difficult for most former business owners. When the ensuing tensions boil over, your employment agreement may be terminated, and if the agreement you signed was not tended to, you may find yourself removed from the company and the employment deal dollars that were part of your buy-out. The other issue about sticking around that could haunt you is the notion that your buy-out is related to the "performance" of the company for a specified period of time. Again, you are not in control, and the "performance" of the company can morph into any number of derivations, so a word of caution is provided here.

In the end, and this is solely my opinion, there is nothing better than taking your cash and walking out the front door. Even if the amount of cash is smaller due to a cash discount paid at the closing, it is far more tolerable and less stressful to take your money and go home. Sometimes "strings attached" can be anchors around your throat, and the benefits of selling the company become severely undermined when your money, and your time, are held hostage.

Where Have You "Missed"?

Here's something else you need to think about. We all have ambitions for our companies and plans we want to see through to fruition, but it doesn't always work that way. It may be that a new product you had such high hopes for falls flat and doesn't grab the customers' attention as you hoped it would. It could even be that your competitors quickly put out a spoiler product, a similar product to yours, reducing the exclusivity of your new introduction.

Alternatively, you could have invested a lot of time and money on a new product in R&D that never got off the ground. Maybe your guys just couldn't get it to work well enough, or you couldn't produce it cheaply enough, so the plan was scrapped.

Whatever it is—however heartbreaking it was—that's another cost of doing business. It cost you money, time, and resources to try new things and seek out new opportunities. The cost of that "miss" may not be limited to money either. You should, of course, know exactly how much money was lost on the venture, but you also need to take into account just what other impacts it could have had on your business.

Perhaps it put the work of your R&D department back six months or a year; perhaps you lost market share to your competitors because you could not update your product or the technology behind your success. Whatever the cost, make note of it and learn from it.

Potential buyers will recognize that every company has a hitch every now and again; just be prepared to stress what positives you have learned from it and how it has made your company better. After all, the new owner should be able to benefit from your misses as well as your successes.

Are You the Industry Leader or a Follower?

Here is a question for you—are you the industry leader or a follower? And why is the question important when it comes to selling your company?

The first thing to realize is that it is actually possible to be both leader and follower at the same time and even on the same project. Everyone always assumes the leader is automatically the one to watch, and often he or she is, *but* there can be benefits in being a follower too.

The business world, for instance, is littered with companies who were at the forefront of invention, the industry leaders in their field, only to be swallowed by the late comers or blown out of the water by their more humble followers. MySpace™ or Friends Reunited™ come to mind in the online space, for instance. In these cases, the followers simply waited for the trailblazers to develop a product, create a market, and generate interest and then simply perfected the product or service in light of the learning curve, swooped in, and took over.

As followers, they didn't have quite the same R&D costs and had the benefit of letting the leader do all the work; they learned from them what worked and what didn't work, they let the industry leader take the risks and pay the costs.

That said, today's leaders tend to share the glory with their followers anyway. Today's business issues are often just too complex for any one heroic leader to figure out. It is fair to say, however, that leaders "influence" others. Natural leaders tend to be competent and socially assertive; they have charisma, and people want to listen when they talk.

Being a leader can have benefits and drawbacks when it comes to a company sale. If you, the owner, are a charismatic mentor and leader of men, you will no doubt have a loyal workforce that strives to make the company a success. That sort of dedicated labor force will be a huge asset to the company and one that any new buyer will want to get their hands on.

It can have a detrimental effect if you are *too* much of a leader, however; if your presence goes beyond just being conducive to your company's success but is actually critical to it. We addressed this in earlier chapters, but it is worth repeating here. A potential buyer isn't going to want to buy your company only for it to fall apart when you leave. If you're the glue or the leader that holds your company together, you're going to have to address it.

Don't be humble or self-effacing; recognize it as a truth *and* as a potential negative. Use the time you have wisely and find yourself another leader or two within your company; encourage the followers to speak up too and create a happy medium within the firm. Suddenly you're not the only one that can lead your company to success; your management team can do it too. Congratulations. The value of your company just increased some more!

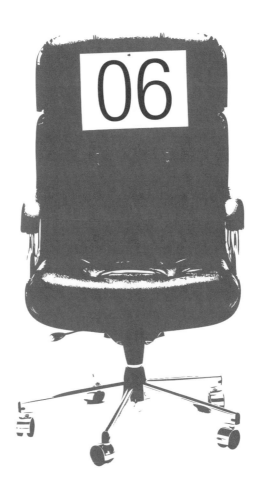

Systems Work When You Don't

McDonald's is a great company! Regardless of whether you like their food or not, they run a great company. If you visit a McDonald's in Las Vegas, Nevada, or one in Sault Ste. Marie, Ontario, Canada, or one anywhere around the world, one thing is very evident—their system allows the company to ensure quality, service, and most importantly, price.

Every business has a system. How you do what you do, when you do it, and who does it makes up your system. If Mary calls in sick, Sue can pick up the pieces to make sure things get done in Mary's absence. Interchangeable people, set processes, same equipment, supportive documentation; systems work and are the backbone to profits. Good businesses know these truths, and they develop their process and then pound it into everyone and everything so that efficiency is maintained.

Here is a question for you: how can systems help you to sell your business?

Everything that we talk about is geared toward helping you understand how an exit strategy can help you sell your business at a fair price that is consistent with the terms you need. I am going to show you just how valuable it is to take a little time out of your day to look in-depth at *how* your business is run, via your systems.

Before I do so, however, let me first clarify what I mean when I mention systems. I don't know about you, but before I first learned about systems, I pictured them a little like a circuit board in a computer: complicated, interconnected, and undefined to the non-expert.

The good news is that systems can actually be very simple. If it helps, picture them as a step-by-step process to complete a particular task to achieve a specific outcome. Namely, a checklist of step-by-step instructions designed to ensure you—or in fact, anyone—gets the right result.

The notion is that systems make everything easier; rather than reinventing the wheel each time you do something, there is already a predetermined course of action to be administered. It's like McDonald's making a hamburger; some customers don't want mustard and some don't want onions, but by far the majority of orders will be for the standard hamburger.

Consider a more germane example. Your customer service department opens an e-mail from a customer who has a question. Your customer service staffer reviews its content and then has to choose from three or four standard e-mails that are already pre-written; they click on the right one, and it gets sent automatically. Bingo. You've answered the customer's query, and you did so while ensuring a set response has been delivered that has been properly vetted.

That's pretty simple, eh? But it's also a process or a business system for customer service, one which helps you to reduce workload, react quicker and consistently, and improve your response to customers. Imagine if your customer service team had to write an e-mail from scratch every single time someone had a query; how long would that take? What might be the quality of the response? Perhaps your customer service representative is having a bad day and provides a response that does not shine your company in the right light.

It's like the elevator analogy. A business without systems is like a building without an elevator; you have to walk, slowly and tediously, up to the 40th floor. It takes a long time, you are tired and no doubt grouchy at the end of it, and you spend so long walking those stairs that you don't have time to do the real work you're supposed to do. Why, oh, why, wouldn't you install an elevator?

In contrast, a company with systems already has the elevator that'll take you — and anyone who wants to get on — straight to the 40th floor. As long as they follow the processes, that elevator will take them to the 40th floor day in and day out, with a minimum of fuss. (It is only when they ignore the processes that it might break down for a day!)

So, what sort of systems are we talking about? How do they work? Well, you are ideally going to want to put systems in place for the four key strategic areas of your business: production, marketing, management, and resources. Of course, there may be several different systems under each of these banners, depending on the exact nature of your company. You may want systems around market research, for instance, accounting, invoicing, deliveries, and more.

Let's go back and consider McDonald's. Each hamburger, millions of them, are made the same way using the same ingredients: a certain amount of ketchup, a set amount of mustard, and the right amount of onions. Each is a known amount, applied the same way by thousands of different employees from every corner of the world. By making it the same way, despite the variability of the workforce, the time of day, or the physical location of the store, McDonald's can operate efficiently and effectively. They know how much ingredients need to be ordered based on the volume produced. They control costs and ensure quality so that every customer that walks through the golden arches has the experience they expect and are more than willing to pay for it. Systems do work, and they work well when properly planned, policed, and processed.

For your business, the idea is to capture winning processes and document them, making them freely accessible so everyone on your staff can learn from them. These processes can take the form of checklists, worksheets, templates, scripts, workflow solutions, question and answer pages…whatever you think works best for the particular task at hand. When applied uniformly, regardless of the staffer performing the task, your business benefits — time and time again.

Would Your Company Benefit From Systems?

I don't even have to know the type of company you own to scream a resounding "YES" to that question. *All* companies can benefit from systems. This is never more evident than when it applies to a business owner. Business owners tend to be busybodies. They always seem to be in a rush. Things around them never seem to move fast enough for their fast-paced appetite. "Get this now, do this now, why isn't this already done?" But yet they just don't want it done; it must be done to their satisfaction, and given the time of day or the day of the week, good luck at trying to figure out what is the right way in their eyes. Is this you? Are you a tyrant one moment and so frustrated that you simply walk away the next? Business owners do not do what they want everyone else to do. This is the sole reason why systems must be established and implemented—so things get done the right way, every day, every time.

As a business owner, if you seem to be always working but never really achieving anything or making much progress, then you need to think about installing some systems into your company.

Even taking just two hours to document a task or a system can free up more vital time in the long-term to do more important tasks. As a result, one of the biggest benefits of systems is that they allow you to see what is mission critical and what isn't. Anything that isn't mission critical can be delegated.

Documenting your business processes and systems is the only surefire way you have of escaping the business now and again. If you're the sort of owner who always needs to be on hand, who ends up working the longest hours of all your employees, who never feels as if you're able to take a day off because everything would ground to a halt without you, you're the problem; you're the one holding your company back from achieving what it can and should—all because you are not leading your company. You are simply making it up each time. That's inefficiency! That's why you are not making the money you think you should. Systems work when the owner doesn't!

Just imagine if the next time someone ran into a problem, they could simply apply the system and would not need to bother you. Or if a new team member had a question about their role, they could just check the documentation instead of waiting to speak to you. Likewise, imagine if a customer complained about service and your team had the confidence to handle the complaint themselves—because you'd given them the power to do so, via set processes or systems; how much time would you save by not firefighting?

The fact is that documenting processes or systems can personally save *you* a lot of time by eliminating many of the daily frustrations and obstacles within your company; the time that it frees up could—and *should*—be used for you to work on your business and not in your business. Perhaps you'd even find the time to begin strategizing your exit strategy. Now there's a novel idea.

Your time is valuable, and you should be dedicating it to those areas where you can have the most strategic input into your company; you shouldn't be dealing with the minutiae of the day.

The point of systems is that, if assessed correctly and applied unilaterally, they should enhance the quality of your service or the performance of your company, and they should free you and key members of your staff to finally begin to address the issues no one ever seems to have time to fix.

Putting the obvious aside for a moment, also note that systems can have a significant positive impact on growing sales. Let's face it; every business only has so much it can devote to business development. As a result, we have to get a return on that investment. Systems can help you measure your performance, assess your return, and aid in deciding what to do next. To make matters a little more convoluted, remember that what works today may not work as your business grows and/or diversifies its products/services. As a business owner, if you are going to invest in something, invest in your systems.

Making sure your employees know what their job is and how it is to be performed will bring about your greatest return on investment.

Document, Document, Document

Let me guess. You started your business as a one-man band and slowly grew to add more employees. You taught those employees how to do their jobs the hands-on way; by working side-by-side with you everything ran smoothly. They then, in turn, helped to train new employees in exactly the same way; everything done by word of mouth.

This evolutionary process is practical and reasonable for a young, growing company. In these instances, the business owner is integral to the business process, as it is important in ensuring the success of the start-up. But as your business grows, its reliance on the owner must decrease. At some point in time, everyone on staff usually has to wait for the owner to make a decision or give direction. It is at these times in your corporate development that business owners have to learn to get out of the way.

You have no doubt heard the stories. The young aspiring entrepreneur starts a new business enterprise and it not only gains traction but also starts to really take off. Wow, the guy is brilliant. It grows and grows, hiring new staffers, diversifying what it does, gaining new customers from far and wide. Then, for some unknown rumor-promulgated reasons, the company begins to struggle. The magic touch seems to have disappeared. The entrepreneur has difficulty motivating the troops. But, then again, the troops know more about the entrepreneur's ability than the outsiders. All of a sudden, in what seems a blink of an eye, the entrepreneur is out. He doesn't run the company anymore; someone else does. Why? Because in many instances the person who is the right one to start the company is not the right one to grow the company. It is almost inevitable; in almost every instance the business owner eventually gets in the way. This is where systems can save the day.

At what point do the hand-me-down processes become outdated? Few small business owners document their processes, but they should; it's the only way to avoid employees creating their own systems or not doing the job in quite the way you envisioned it being done. Each time a task is reinvented, your labor dollars are being wasted. Each time a task is reinvented, your quality control is being challenged and your company is at greater risk. When your staff is small, you can manage each person. This simplistic approach is effective, and it helps create your business brand. Your mission becomes more defined, and its purpose is practiced. But at some point, you begin to miss the point. You can only manage a larger pool of employees through systems. Handholding is out. Coddling is out. Hoping someone does what they are supposed to do is out. Systems help you extend the mission of your company.

But there is another point-of-view worth noting. From a business owners perspective, the lack of systems puts you at risk. You see, at some point almost every business ends up developing one, or at the very most, a few rising stars. These are staffers who really make a difference in the performance of the company. These rising stars get it, and you depend on them. But just like everything in life, the pendulum swings the other way, and these rising stars begin to understand their own power—and they flaunt it. At first, the business owner allows it to happen because the rising star's performance and the company's reliance are synonymous. Each needs the other. But there comes a point when the rising star's attitude begins to undermine the pervasive attitude of the company. Challenges erupt; bad things begin to happen. The business owner is held hostage because he/she has come to rely on the performance of the rising star. Allowing a staffer to pursue their own "unique" way of working gets to be a problem, even for the most liberal business owners.

Documenting the processes of your business allows you to manage the outcomes. The people implementing the process become interchangeable. Regardless of which staffer sits in which chair, assuming the processes are administered by a capable individual (*and* the processes are right in the first place), the results should always be predictable.

At the same time, those systems and processes can work when you *don't*. Whenever you're out of the office, sleeping, taking a well-earned day off or a vacation, those systems can still operate. Some of them may be automated and will work no matter what time of the day or night, while others may rely on other people following your exact procedures. Either way, those self-same systems and processes keep your business operating, even when you're not there.

How to Create Efficiency

If I've convinced you of the need for systems, just where should you start and how? Looking around your company you may see any number of areas that could benefit from enhanced organizational control. But how do you determine where to start?

Start simple and start small. Every company can be

divided into three fundamental areas: *administration, business development, and operations*. Pick the three most important tasks performed in each of the three aforementioned areas. Prioritize the three tasks in each of the three areas. Start with the top-ranked task in each category because, chances are, they are all related. If you try to do everything at once, you are only going to end up tired and frustrated, and eventually you will simply give up.

Once you have prioritized your tasks, the easiest way to document or generate your systems is not to try to create them from scratch but instead to document what you, or your staff, are already doing. Next, review all the processes and edit them if needed. You will no doubt find tasks that are being done incorrectly or inefficiently, others that duplicate work done elsewhere, and still others that cause potential problems for customers and other third-party individuals.

Always keep in mind what the outcome should be. What does success look like, and what are the key milestones? Likewise, if a step finishes at a certain point without follow-up, what should the next step be? (If you don't close a sales deal, for instance, how do you follow up? What is to be learned from the failure, and how does this information get channeled into the next proposal?) Be specific; remember the step-by-step processes should make sense to anyone who doesn't know the company as well as you do.

Your system documentation needs to be available and accessible to everyone; adaptable — use some form of document control to allow users (either all users or elected individuals) to edit and delete obsolete information; easily searchable (the information needs to be at their fingertips); and secure (to protect your intellectual property).

A good system should take into account the process itself and the interdependencies (components) needed to help it function efficiently. I've been using the words "system" and "process" as if they are interchangeable throughout this description, and to some extent they are. The process is best defined as the strategic approach (as viewed from 10,000 feet), while the system should be classified as the tactic (what is done in the trenches). Without effective processes, your business systems would not exist.

Good processes should be effective and standardized, saving you money and ensuring your brand. Systems should eliminate mistakes, idle time, bottlenecks, downtime, and adverse regulatory and/or legal impacts.

Remember, a system is only as good as its component parts. There is no point installing a system when missing equipment, checklists, supplies, tools, or other resources make it impossible to function.

Don't sidestep this part of the system; missing or poor quality components are often the downfall of small businesses. If you don't address the lack of components, you are hamstringing your staff before they even begin. What is most important in all of this is how your employees view the system. If it is not important to you the owner, it assuredly will not be important to them.

You will need the right people in the right jobs for the right reason in order to make this work. Ensure you offer the right training, take time to answer questions, and most importantly, be flexible when an employee identifies a shortcoming in the system and offers a fix. If employees believe in the system, they will follow the system. Having a system in place can help a good worker become an exceptional employee achieving exceptional results.

Finally, your systems should identify ways to boost quality and increase speed; you don't want bottlenecks, wasted time, or reworking and neither do you want defects or poor-quality, inferior goods. The latter will turn customers away who will never come back, while the former will cost you money.

The good news is that if you have the right systems in place, you can boost quality and productivity and increase capacity and customer satisfaction while also reducing mistakes and costs at the same time! Just don't forget to instigate measurements to track your systems. You'll want to know how your new processes are contributing to your larger business goals.

How Systems Sell Your Business

Now we get to the rub; why am I telling you about systems. What on earth does it have to do with the topic of this book—creating an exit strategy and selling at the price you need to ensure you protect, and are ready for, the next stage of your life?

Systems will influence the potential sale of your business. In fact, systems can have a significant impact on the value of your business and the attractiveness it has to a prospective purchaser.

You see, I can practically guarantee you that buyers are looking for businesses that have effective business systems. They want to see systems and processes in place that have been shown to work, producing consistently good results on quality, efficiency, and profitability. They are likely to place significant emphasis on business systems as you begin to negotiate the value of your business.

A company without well-documented and organized systems is going to look haphazard. For the same reasons we talked about business owners being a logjam or a rising star holding a company hostage, these are the same issues a potential purchaser wants to avoid. Perception is the reality, and for business buyers, what a business looks like, how it seems to operate, and how it makes its money are the perceptions that lead to perceived value. Companies are bought and sold every day based on perceived value. An educated buyer, those likely to pay you a premium for your business, will conduct necessary due diligence. They will ask the tough questions and review the documentation. Effective use of systems can bring a return on your investment because buyers will always pay for value.

A company that has its systems in place has taken the time to examine its administrative, sales development, and operational functions. This investment is a great selling proposition and makes your company much more appealing to potential buyers.

One last thing. Recall the time horizon we talked about in an earlier chapter. It takes time to prepare you and your company for sale. Most companies need time to fix the things that haven't been a primary focus over the last several years. By focusing on effective systems, not only can the company reduce its dependency on you, but it can make more money while you are preparing for a sale. Having the right systems in place is a moneymaker.

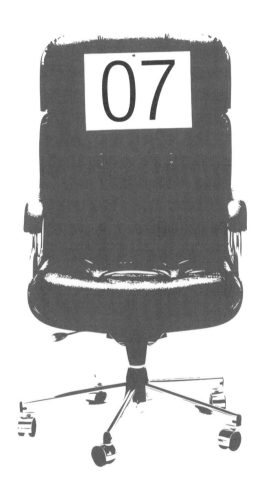

Forget Chapter 6: What Really Sells a Company?

Okay, let's get down to the real nitty-gritty. Take everything I told you in Chapter 6 and throw it away! We're going to discuss the issues that will really sell your business.

Before you go crazy on me, let me clarify something first. Everything presented in Chapter 6 IS important. It's all true! Buyers want to see that you have systems in place to allow the company to grow. They want to see systems that do not put all the power or leverage into one or a few employees' hands. They want to be assured that when you walk away into the sunset after the sale, the business will continue to perform, and its customers will remain loyal to the brand and not you. YES, Chapter 6 is important, but Chapter 7 is MORE important.

Let's put all of this in context before we start. Chapter 6 is frosting on the cake. It's appreciated by buyers, but when it comes down to it, it's just adding color and pizzazz on top of the solid foundation—the cake. What really sells the company is what's under the frosting…namely, the actual cake. If the cake itself isn't strong enough or appealing enough to a buyer, it doesn't matter how great the frosting is because the business won't sell.

Have you ever bitten into a gorgeous-looking cake only to discover the frosting is good, but the cake itself is tasteless? Perhaps you prefer chocolate cake, but when you cut into it, yikes, it is sponge cake. Maybe it has lemon in it and you just *hate* lemon.

Isn't it disappointing?

Wouldn't it be great if you could get great frosting and cake together?

Although the analogy of the cake and its semblance to your business is simple, the relationship between the cake and the frosting is very tangible. Every business has its internal and external workings. What the business looks like is the frosting; how the business works is the cake. Just like connoisseurs of great tasting cakes, business buyers are always interested in companies that look good on the outside and work well on the inside. Is one more important than the other? Of course! In this instance, Chapter 7 is more important than Chapter 6, but both are still important.

With regard to the underlying performance of your company, we could spend numerous pages discussing how effective strategic planning, communications, continuous improvement, and operational efficiency are key to a well run company. In fact, there are hundreds of books on this very topic, and although vitally important, suffice it to say that this book is not aimed at teaching you what you have to do to optimize the performance of your company. We will leave that to other books and other authors.

The Exit Equation is aimed at giving you specific insights as to how to go about planning and executing your greatest deal ever—the sale of your business. With this said, the focus of this chapter is "what really sells your company." So, as we move into the heart of this chapter, it is important to note there are two fundamental components (and no, it is not frosting and cake) a buyer will be looking at above all else when it comes to deciding whether to buy a business: terms and cash.

Start With the Easy One: Terms

Terms are often driven by the buyer's need for assurances, and you, as the seller, have to find a way to provide the assurance they need. A business for the right price but with the wrong terms is a deal worth walking away from.

Here's a shocker—the price you might be asking for your business does not dictate the value of the deal. Terms drive price. If you have caught on to one of the underlying messages of *The Exit Equation* thus far, you should be starting to realize the asking price is not what you should be focusing on; you should always focus on what you want and need after you leave and how the terms of the sale may impede that goal.

The seemingly ironic aspect of terms over price centers on the belief by most business buyers that the current owner is more interested in how much money needs to change hands to make the deal work. Everyone knows that money makes the world go round, and when negotiating the sale of a business, everything centers on money, doesn't it? It is this common misconception that gives you, the seller, an advantage over the buyer. In fact, it's one of the few distinct advantages you will have in the negotiating process, so you better learn how to leverage it.

1. What are you selling?

The broader, seemingly most pertinent term of the deal is the simple notion of exactly what you are selling. Which assets are to be included with the sale of the company, and which assets are to remain with you? When you take all your corporate assets, both tangible and intangible, each represents a certain value to you and to the buyer. In a microcosm, they are not nearly as valuable individually as they may be collectively. So the key is for you to pre-arrange the combination of key corporate assets, making sure the buyer understands the synergistic value of certain asset bundles and why other assets "probably" are not important. I use the word "probably" only in the context that certain assets may have more value to you than to the buyer. If the buyer does not need these assets, keep them to yourself for potential future use.

Let's start with tangible and intangible assets. Tangible assets are obvious: property, buildings, equipment, fixtures, vehicles, tools, existing contracts, accounts receivable, subsidiary companies, and inventory are examples of tangible assets. These are easily quantifiable and value-determined. In almost all circumstances, these are integral to the operation of the business. Intangible assets, on the other hand, are generally not critical to the business and are almost always de-valued by the buyer in some respect. Intangible assets might include life insurance policies, specific client/customer relationships (more on this shortly), cell phone numbers, intellectual property, deposits (e.g., utility, specific services), bank relationships, and related collateral.

All assets should be reviewed and prioritized prior to contract negotiations. As mentioned earlier, pre-arranging obvious combinations of key corporate assets and the synergies these assets bring to the benefit of the buyer will be beneficial in supporting your asking price. The key here is to determine which assets might not be needed and whether these present any value to you. For instance, intellectual property generally includes trade secrets (e.g., customer lists), copyrights, patents, and trademarks, as well as competitive intangibles, such as collaboration activities and leverage options.

Perhaps some of these assets are not likely to be of value to the prospective buyer, and if so, presenting a reasonable argument as to why they do not need to be incorporated into the transaction makes sense; especially if these assets have a future value to you. Remember, always take into account what you intend to do following the sale. If you have a strong desire to pursue another business or even a glorified hobby, maybe some of these assets will be useful to you.

Some tangible assets worth keeping are more of a personal nature. For instance, your office computer, laptop, personal digital assistant device, cell phone, pager, and other similar equipment are always worth keeping. Your argument is that this equipment inherently has some personal information on it, and you'd like to keep it in your possession. Buyers usually will be agreeable to these types of requests. Take life insurance policies for instance. If you used a life insurance policy as a means of funding a Capital Stock Buy/Sell Agreement, chances are the policy is of no value to the buyer. If the policy is a term policy and has no cash value, a buyer is likely willing to assign the policy to you.

Another simple example is your cell phone number. Because these numbers can now be transferred between carriers, it only makes sense for you to keep your number. Friends, family, business acquaintances, and other business representatives all have your number, so it is obvious that unless you want to reestablish contact with all these folks under a new cell phone number, you might as well keep it.

The buyer does not need it, and it brings no value to the deal.

The same is true for monetary deposits paid to utility companies and specific service providers and rent and leased equipment deposits. If paid in your corporate name, these may be refundable to you as part of the new owner establishing his own account.

As for bank relationships and related collateral, simply keep in mind that your banking deals will need to be settled as part of any pending sale. Apart from the obviousness of paying off any term or revolving debt, there are always other banking issues to resolve, including credit card debt, lien rights, and release of collateral to name a few.

How much of the purchase price do you get at closing?

First and foremost, find out how the buyer intends to fund the sale. It is a simple enough question, and if you really want to favorably position yourself for negotiations, ask the question and ask it early. As briefly discussed in an earlier chapter, it is always better to get your money lump sum and walk out the door. There are no ensuing theatrics, no bad blood, no second-guessing. If the buyer wants you to stay on but you'd rather leave and he agrees to a lump sum buy-out in exchange for a cash discount, I recommend you seriously consider the discount and walk out the front door. You will never regret cash in the bank; you will regret having to wait to get your cash.

If it is an installment sale (e.g., land contract) or if the buyer wants you to agree to some kind of earn-out where the amount of money you get is based on the future performance of the company, these deals are wrought with manipulated metrics, lack of direct ability to influence performance because of a lack of control, and inclusion of non-essential expenses that adversely impact the bottom line and your wallet. Should you be compelled to accept an offer in this context, get as much as you can at the closing and consider how the pay-out is classified. Your tax advisor may want you to take most of the payment in the form of salary in lieu of a stock buy-back (ordinary income versus capital gain). The key in all of this is to find out if the buyer is bankable and, if so, by whom. Financing a corporate purchase is often tricky for both the banker and the seller.

To what extent will you remain involved in the company after the sale?

Back in Chapter 4, I mentioned that you may be asked to stay on as a consultant for a period of time. In many instances, some portion of the sales price is tied to your continued participation. If you are not in control of the company, and its "performance" is a condition of the sales price, look out.

There is nothing better than taking your cash and walking out the front door, even if the amount is smaller due to a cash discount paid at the closing. Always remember, "strings attached" can be anchors around your neck, and the benefits of selling the company become severely undermined when your money and your time are held hostage.

If you are not asked to stay on, then your focus needs to turn to the importance of your specific client/customer relationships. As is often the case, a buyer is going to want to limit your opportunity to serve an existing client/customer. Usually packaged into a Non-Compete Agreement, these limitations can be significant. Buyers may require these agreements for a variety of reasons, including protection of trade secrets or goodwill. However, courts generally disapprove of Non-Compete Agreements as limitations on a former employee's right to earn a living.

It is important to note, in order to be considered valid, a Non-Compete Agreement must:

- Be supported by consideration at the time it is signed;
- Protect a legitimate business interest of the new business owner; and
- Be reasonable in scope, geography, and time.

These agreements must generally be supported by valid consideration—the seller must receive something of value in exchange for the promise to refrain from competition. Such additional consideration may consist of cash, cash-equivalents (e.g., equipment, cash-value insurance policies) or another additional benefit that is not part of the Purchase Agreement.

When considering your relationship with a particular client/customer, the goodwill developed by you in terms of customer relations is an asset, so a buyer may use a Non-Compete Agreement to prevent you from capitalizing on that goodwill. Also, a prospective buyer may use an agreement to protect its confidential information. In these instances, the buyer must show that it took reasonable measures to keep the information secret and that the information gives the buyer a competitive advantage.

Non-Compete Agreements must also be reasonable in terms of duration and scope. The reasonableness of the duration of the agreement will depend on the specific facts of each case. If the agreement is designed to protect confidential information, the duration should be no longer than the time for which the information has value. My suggestion is that if you are compelled to enter into such an agreement, do so by limiting the duration to no more than two years. My argument to your buyer is that you intend to retire, and once you are off the shelf for two years, your ability to compete is substantively lost.

In terms of geographic location, the area covered by the agreement must also be reasonable since courts will not allow a Non-Compete Agreement to prevent an employee from working in a geographical area where the prospective purchaser does not do business. Again, my argument is that if the business is not currently competing in a particular area, then it should not be a limiting condition of what you might do in the future.

You should note there are significant tax implications involving compensation under Non-Compete Agreements. Payments under these agreements are considered a legitimate business expense. The question, though, is whether you can take the expense in one year or whether you must amortize it over several years. In a 2010 Tax Court case[4], a company paid $400,000 to a former employee for a one-year covenant not to compete. The Tax Court ruled that even though the agreement was for one year, the Non-Compete Agreement was an intangible asset defined in Section 197 of the Internal Revenue Code, and it must be amortized over 15 years. This could prove to be a significant issue to a seller so it is best to be prepared and knowledgeable as to how these agreements works and what their tax implications will be on you. Remember, if you must sign an agreement make sure the agreement stipulates how much of the sales price is specifically linked to the Non-Compete Agreement.

---

4 http://www.ustaxcourt.gov/InOpHistoric/recoverygroup.TCM.WPD.pdf

Non-Compete Agreements are certainly not new, but anecdotally they appear to be gaining interest as a means of protecting a company's ability to operate and compete. There is much information on this important topic, so you are strongly encouraged to refrain from entering into one of these agreements. If you must, speak with an experienced tax advisor and attorney to ensure your legal rights are protected and the impact on your wallet is fully understood.

How will tax considerations affect your net proceeds from the sale?

As a business owner, you are all too familiar with the impact the tax man has on your bank account. With the advent of the sale of your business, the tax man will reach even further into your personal wallet to take his fair share, so it becomes important for you to consider how the terms of any pending deal are stipulated. There are plenty of business books in the market that present a detailed accounting of how the tax man will participate in your deal, so I will leave that discussion to the tax professionals. Suffice it to say, the amount the tax man will take from you will likely be substantial, so talk to an expert tax advisor as your negotiations evolve. It is money very well spent.

General Advice About Negotiating Terms

Some business advisors say that you should obtain a business broker or intermediary do all your negotiating for you—that you should not talk directly with the buyer until almost everything has been settled. The argument is that a broker may be better able to remain objective without giving too much away. Other business advisors say you are the best representative of your company and of your own expectations from the sale, and buyers will respond better to direct contact with you.

This is an important consideration and although each side has compelling arguments, my suggestion is to rely on your instincts. There are those business owners who are superb salespeople and are best prepared to close the deal. On the contrary, some business owners are simply too emotionally attached to their businesses and are not likely to be logical when negotiating the pros and cons of your business and its resultant value. The size and price range of your business may also play a part in your decision, since brokers are paid on commission.

Another recommendation: keep the lawyers out of the way until you arrive at some general agreement with the buyer. Lawyers certainly serve an important purpose, but they are paid by the hour and often get consumed with minutiae that, in the end, may not pose an unreasonable risk. But remember, condition your early discussions and any general agreements on the proviso that your accountant and tax advisor need to be apprised of the situation and the details. After the Letter of Intent is executed, there is plenty of time for the respective attorneys to quibble over the details.

Now, the Hard One: Cash

No matter if this is their first business purchase or their twentieth, a buyer is always looking for one thing—an on-going income. They are interested in a company with a proven track record—one that demonstrates a consistent financial performance and solid/growing revenues and earnings.

Business buyers are attracted to potential businesses because of a variety of perceived benefits and synergies. Maybe they have seen your business operate from afar and believe in its mission. Perhaps a buyer has a complimentary business and yours would be the perfect fit whereby one plus one equals ten. It could be they believe the market is ripe for growth and your business has great potential to benefit from a growth spurt.

Regardless of the reasons for the initial attraction, once they get through the frosting, they will get down to the cake, and if the bottom line is what they believe, their interest becomes compelling.

Never underestimate how important cash flow and profitability are to a buyer; that is why we've already talked about presenting your cash flow statements in as appealing a way as possible. Your job is to make sure they are aware of the potential your company has ahead of itself and how that potential can play to the benefit of the owner.

It is important to note that business buyers can easily be classified into two categories: *inexperienced* and *experienced*.

An inexperienced buyer will place immense value on proven financial performance. They are buying your profit-making machine. Although they want to be comfortable with the ancillary aspects of the business—corporate image, staff, book of business, equipment, and growth potential—most put heavy reliance on the business' ability to generate cash. Remember, they are inexperienced when it comes to business operations or business purchases, so their view is usually laser focused because they think price is the most important issue to you because it is to them. Use this misconception to your advantage. Make sure you recast your earnings to make the company sparkle in the perfect world perception of the would-be buyer. Lay it on thick with sound financial documents to back it up. You'd be surprised how many business owners try to sell their company with shoddy paperwork or poor financial records. It's as if they hope the potential buyer will take it on faith that the business is a good one. It's no wonder only 30% of small businesses sell.

As for experienced buyers, I have a theory, which has often proved accurate. I believe experienced buyers are not nearly as interested in highly efficient, high-performing eight-cylinder companies as they are with companies that are operating on only six or seven cylinders. Experienced buyers are buying "potential"; they realize the purchase price will be paid by the efficiency and profit improvements that result from post-sale changes to the company. Remember, business buyers, especially experienced business buyers, are entrepreneurs. By their nature entrepreneurs are business builders; they live for the challenge to do what others say cannot be done.

So when you find yourself sitting down across the table from an experienced business buyer, remember to view them as an entrepreneur. They are more interested in the potential your company has to grow than they are in its cash-generating ability (although cash is always important). As a result, your overall strategy needs to be centered on this changing buyer expectation and your corresponding tactics need to play to the buyer's wants and needs.

When it comes to the question of what your company is worth, keep in mind that a vast majority of all deals must cash flow. Inevitably you are enamored with your business and have poured years of invaluable sweat equity into its coffers. You inherently believe the risk-return curve now favors you and the value of your company fits perfectly into some business valuation formula. Good luck meeting your expectation! Chances are your perfect-world valuation formula does not cash flow. It is only in those rare instances when a buyer will actually pay a premium for a business; all others must be bankable.

I recently served a business owner who had been approached to sell her business. As similarly presented in the preceding paragraphs, she created her business from scratch and made it work. Her investments in time and capital resources were substantial; the business served her personal interests, and she operated it as such. She had two would-be buyers solicit her—one an experienced buyer and one inexperienced. Both had been attracted to the business because of its perceived value and competitive advantage.

The inexperienced buyer focused on the cash flow aspects of the deal, appearing not to be overly interested in how the business could grow. The buyer was concerned about cash flow validity and was willing to meet the seller's asking price. It sounded great at the time, but the problem was the buyer and the bankability of the deal. In the end, a financing deal could not be structured because the deal was too expensive and would not cash flow. Yes, the seller got her asking price, and yes, the buyer was expecting to get a cash-generating machine that ensured the bank note would be paid, but neither the inexperienced buyer nor the money hungry seller won out in the end. The seller was obviously disappointed, but the result was to be expected, and she was advised of this likely outcome in advance.

With regard to the experienced buyer, this deal was similar to the general expectations presented earlier in this chapter.

The buyer was more interested in the potential growth of the business and structured a deal supported by the cash flow of the business. The offer price was significantly lower than the inexperienced buyer's offer, but the deal was bankable and financing was secured. The offer met all of the seller's terms but was rejected because the price was too low. Even though the baby boomer-aged seller was very eager to sell and would walk away with a lump sum amount of cash in her pocket, she could not understand how her personal interests and the way she operated the company had an adverse impact on her asking price.

These situations are not uncommon. Business owners typically over-value their businesses. What they fail to realize is that they tend to operate their businesses in a manner that supports their personal lifestyle more than in a manner that grows return on investment and value. Yes, it is absolutely their decision, and they have every right to exercise their control. But remember, when you put your business on the sales block, any pending purchaser is going to see the company as you have structured and operated it. If your decision on the structure and operation of your business puts your personal interests ahead of the company, do not be surprised if the value of your company is less than you think. Think of it this way...

> *"The buyer rarely buys what the seller thinks he's selling."*
> **Management guru, Peter Drucker**

As mentioned in earlier chapters of *The Exit Equation*, if you are going to enjoy the fruits of your labor and risk-taking, you need to fix the issues which adversely affect a sale. In the case of my previous example, the business owner wasted two opportunities because the gravitational force of a potential sale preempted the needed process of adequately preparing the company, and the owner, for a sale.

When it comes right down to it, the "science" of selling your company is all about cash and terms—nothing more, nothing less. The "art" of the sale is for you to know it is time to go, why you are going, and what you are going to be faced with when you get there. We've only touched on this important topic thus far; there's more to come.

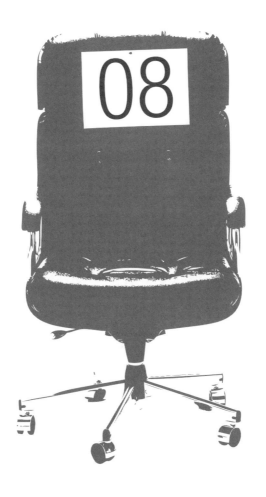

Willing Buyers & Willing Sellers: Follow the Yellow Brick Road

In recent years, and certainly into the foreseeable future, business sellers are no longer in the driver's seat. If you don't believe me or if you think your business might be special, consider the simple law of supply and demand.

In the next five to ten years, baby boomer-aged business owners in the U.S. will sell over 12,000,000 companies in order to retire. When you consider recent census data monitored by the U.S. Small Business Administration, there are some 27.5 million businesses operating in the U.S. each year. Factor in about a 10% annual turnover rate, and that is the number of companies that close each year less the number of new companies entering the market. You will concur that baby boomer-aged businesses not only make up a significant percentage of the companies in the country, but the supply of available businesses for sale will wreak havoc in how supply/demand lines reach equilibrium.

As they say, it is a buyer's market.

Baby Boomers are defined as the group of people born between 1946 and 1964. This group of 77 million Americans accounts for 28% of the population, according to Baby Boomer Headquarters[5].

---

5 http://www.bbhq.com/

Baby boomer-aged business owners think that selling their business at the right time could be a means to obtain the funds needed to maintain a comfortable retirement lifestyle. Their need to liquefy assets is likely underscored by the fact that Baby Boomers are considered a generation of poor savers. Recent research suggests the majority of Baby Boomers will not have sufficient funds to retire when they hit the traditional retirement age of 65.

With these realities as a backdrop, it is no wonder that creating an exit strategy is more critical than ever, and learning how to tactically navigate the process can be your greatest professional challenge.

Willing Buyers, Willing Sellers and Fair Market Value

What is fair? What you consider fair may be a slap in the face to the prospective buyer sitting across the table from you. Likewise, the price offered by a would-be purchaser of your business may not even come close to compensating you for the years of sweat equity and risk-taking you endured to get your business off the ground and running successfully. Quantitatively, there is no magic formula; qualitatively, there is. Fair market value results when willing buyers and willing sellers meet in the middle.

Your willingness to sell and someone else's willingness to buy is premised on logic and consensus. Logic comes from data and reasonable expectation balanced against acceptable risk. Consensus is derived from the ideal that no one loses; everyone wins. So how do we get there?

Price Versus Value

As briefly discussed in Chapter 7, there's a typical mistake business owners make when thinking of selling a business—*they confuse price with value*. It's important that you realize the two are not the same, neither are they interchangeable.

Price and value are very different for one simple reason: the *price* of your business is simply what someone is willing to pay for it, while the *value* of your business, in contrast, is what your business is actually worth. So, it could be said that value comes at a price. When the root factors of this idiom are out of sync, as is the case when price does not support the value of a business, we are said to be in a buyer's market.

Time and time again, business sellers rack their brains to come up with what they see as the all-important price for their business, only to later regret how the sum was derived because setting the price too early in negotiations is a deal killer. How can you ask for a realistic price if you haven't yet worked out what your company is really worth; if you haven't yet established its value? In this context, the price comes from value, and value is the definition of what all the pieces are worth.

Ideally, you have a value in mind and, in fact, if you are like most business owners, this value comes from various mathematical calisthenics you and your accountant perform each year. Knowing your corporate valuation not only helps you sell your business, it also helps you take advantage of opportunities that may come your way unexpectedly.

Let's consider what the ingredients are when deriving your company's value.

How to Value Your Company

There are several ways you can establish value. Simply put, the valuation of a business is determining its worth using objective methods—and there are various methods that you can use here—to evaluate all aspects of your business.

So what sort of things should you be including in your valuation (whichever manner of valuation you use)? You're going to need to look at your company's capital structure, assets, future earning potential, client base, management system, assumptions/limitations, economic outlook for the industry, prospects for growth, potential threats, and of course, the financial data to back it all up.

In the context of determining a corporate valuation, I will always defer to an expert. Experienced accountants who possess specific corporate valuation expertise are the experts to whom I refer. These folks have a wealth of information at their disposal involving specific trade data, sales histories and comparables, financial ratios, tax law, and acceptable accounting principles. These experts provide the details and industry-specific information needed to determine what valuation method applies best to your industry and business and can guide you through the typical accounting nuances to derive a value that is defensible. I offer the following summary merely to give you a sense of the intangibles and importance of the process.

Assets: It's easy to think that assets only include tangible, physical objects—land, buildings, factories, equipment, furniture, and fixtures. However, there is more to assets than simply what you can see and touch. Intangible assets often play a huge role in valuing your business. Issues that include brand loyalty, employees and your corporate expertise, and your business development process bring a substantial value to your business.

Client/Customer Base: This is often an enormous component of value. Let's face it; people do business with who they trust. Treat them fairly and bring value to the transaction, and your clients/customers are likely to support your asking price.

Prospects for Growth: A record of steady profits and strong orders going forward will certainly help your valuation. The higher your profits and the more aptitude your company has to grow its sales, the greater the value.

Industry Outlook: How your company and your industry are doing is another indicator of the value of your business. If it's in a lively market with potential for growth as an industry, it's going to be much more valuable to a potential buyer. Conversely, if your industry is dying or the community you call home is struggling, your corporate value will be less.

As you can see, everything your company touches and everything that touches your company are value indicators. Your path along the yellow brick road includes the industry and market in which you compete; the political leanings and economic development efforts of the state and community you call home; and the way you aid and support your staff.

Value is the relative worth, merit, or importance of each component of your company. That's why you have to take the emotion out of it and rationally value your business; don't value it on what it means to you personally but on how strong a company it is in the real world.

Yes, you want enough money to begin your retirement and the next phase of your life knowing that you will be comfortable, but over-valuing a company is never going to get you there. All over-valuing does is price you out of the market and leave you without any willing buyers.

Once you have a value, determine your terms and then, and only then, set the price. Remember, only 30% of small businesses sell. A great many of those who don't sell are simply asking for too much money.

Forget a Magic Formula

When it comes to price, let me just give you a couple of pointers. The first thing to realize is there is no magic formula for determining the asking price for your company. How you determine a valuation may be fair and reasonable to you but it doesn't mean your analyses will be accepted by the buyer. I still contend price plays a backseat to terms. Get the terms you want and the price takes care of itself.

Another suggestion has to do with expectation. At the onset of discussions, talk to the prospective buyer and ask a lot of questions. Don't be mesmerized by the buyer's interest in your company, and it is highly recommended you keep your exuberance to a minimum. Find out why they want to buy and what they want out of the company once they get it. These answers will be tremendous assets to you in formulating your terms and setting your asking price.

My third point relative to price centers on the bankability of the deal. If you're asking price is not bankable—if it does not cash flow—the deal is likely dead on arrival. If you want a deal that is non-bankable, you will likely have to carry some or all of the note. This is where the risk/return lines start to become blurry. This is why at the outset of this book we talk about pursuing a retrospective view as to why you want to leave your company and under what conditions. The exit strategy process alone is pitted with landmines: emotions, perception, ego-stroking, and honor. These pitfalls all come at the seller's expense and a lack of a plan only magnifies their importance. Couple this with the fact that you might find yourself in a buyer's market, and the challenges of not having an exit strategy become cataclysmic.

So if you are the seller, how do you combat the rising odds against you? Remember that the sale process typically has multiple steps: financial appraisal and assessment of value; marketing the business; locating a prospective buyer; structuring the transaction; managing the buyer due diligence; and negotiating and closing the transaction and post-close transaction. Despite the importance of having a clear-cut plan in place when deciding to sell, according to a survey of small business owners by *M&A Today* 65% of business owners do not know what their company is worth and 85% have no exit strategy. Worse yet, many business owners fix a price in their mind and may directly or indirectly communicate that price to potential buyers and competitors.

Are You Pricing Your Company Out of the Market?

It's easy to do; you've worked hard on building your business from the ground up, so of course you want a good price for it. You just can't understand why other people can't see it for the great opportunity it is. Or maybe you've done the hard work of valuing your business, justifying the value of each segment of the company and taking the emotion out of it, but now a buyer tells you it's just too much money. But you're only asking what the company is worth, so why should you lower the price?

Buyers too can have unrealistic expectations. Consider a buyer who is looking for an income stream but wants to pay the lowest price possible. He's going to think your company isn't worth anything more than he wants to pay for it. In this situation, the buyer doesn't see value; he wants a deal. What are the odds you can change his perspective? Do you think you can get him to increase his offering? If you are compelled to sell; if you really want to get out; if you haven't really invested time to fix your business and set a realistic value; if you become mesmerized at the dollars a sale could bring, then you are doomed. In this scenario the buyer is playing you. The buyer is pitting your emotion and poor planning to their advantage. Business owners who are quick to sell are usually the ones who get caught up in the euphoria of the sale and usually sell themselves short.

Start with the end in mind and understand what you need in the sale and work the process backwards as we have pronounced in this book. It is imperative you put yourself first, deciding what you need from the sale and on what terms. Recognize that your company has likely served your needs over the last several years, and the more you have taken out of it, the less it is worth today. For many of you, consign yourselves to the reality that you have not managed your company for profits and growth but rather to fit your lifestyle. If this is you, then take some time to refocus what you want from your company when you decide to leave and prepare it for your departure. In the end, it is the reality and effort that will best serve your needs. On the flip side of the "deal" buyer, consider the opportunity of selling to someone who wants your business to support a certain lifestyle. These are folks who are more interested in business location, profit growth, future security, and the industry. They see value and are willing to pay for it because they are getting something more than just cash flow and realize there is a price to pay for these benefits/amenities.

How do you determine who is a "price buyer" and who is a "lifestyle buyer"? In many instances, all you have to do is ask the questions and listen to the answers. For the first time in probably a long time, you do not have all the answers and you do not know for certain what the buyer is thinking or wanting. Check your ego at the door, sit down, and listen. This is where your planning and patience will to pay off Inevitably, the buyer will tell you what you need to know, so ask the questions.

At some point the process turns to price, and when it does, be reasonable and flexible. Each prospective buyer comes to the table with their own strategy and a willingness to pay a certain amount of money dictated by their needs and wants. If the buyer wants what you are selling, good things happen. If you have not prepared yourself and your company for a sale, you will probably have to live with what will turn out to be your greatest regret.

Consummated deals are the result of willing buyers and willing sellers coming to a consensus. Listen to what the buyer wants out of the deal; if you think negotiations are worth your time then formulate the terms you want—and then talk price. All of this can be boiled down to the simple notion that if you plan your work and work your plan, good things will happen.

Deal-Making

While it's true that fewer business-for-sale deals are being made during the current recession, it's not because potential buyers aren't looking. Across the country, there is plenty of buy interest in businesses, but a shortage of financing is keeping many deals from getting off the ground. As a result, sellers willing to finance at least part of a business sale are finding it much easier to get their businesses sold.

By offering seller financing, a business seller allows a buyer to make a down payment, agreeing to carry a note for the remainder of the purchase price. This way, the buyer only has to come up with a portion of the total price up front and can then pay off the remainder over time.

A seller's willingness to finance a portion of a business sale has always been a strong selling point for potential buyers. But in recent months it has become essential to many deals. With most business buyers unable to access the full amount of a business price from lending institutions, today's sellers are faced with the decision to either lower asking prices or work with buyers to overcome sale barriers.

As mentioned a number of times in this book, as a seller one of your jobs is to find out how the buyer intends to pay you for your company. Consequently, knowledge of how financing options fit into the overall picture and being flexible with these options can make the difference if a deal will ever reach the closing table. The most common financing methods include bank financing, owner financing, and conditional performance notes.

Bank Financing: The Old Is New Again

Getting a business loan is not as convenient or as flexible as it used to be. Just a few short years ago, money was prevalent. Loans were made on the status of accounts receivable, personal guarantees, and the value of your collateral. Leverage was the rage since you could buy almost anything and sell it for more. Banking was easy, and getting loans was easier. But the presumption of success became the pivot point for economic malaise. As fast as things went up, they came down faster. Once the home mortgage bubble burst and the economy began its freefall, money standards tightened considerably; now we find ourselves back to the old ways—at least 20% down, significant collateral coverage, and reliance on solid personal and corporate financial statements.

The Federal Reserve has recently stated that banks have eased their lending standards for small businesses for the first time in nearly four years (remember, by definition "small business" is defined as those with annual sales less than $50 million). Is this really the case? Of course not! The Federal Reserve readily admits the easing of credit standards is limited to large domestic banks. Small regional banks continue to struggle and, for those who claim they are not struggling, ask them if their lending standards have changed. Of course they have.

Bank financing is available, but it is harder to get if the deal does not meet stringent standards. The more unrealistic your demands as a seller, even if the buyer agrees, the more likely the deal will not get financed. Another tripping hazard is the buyer. If the deal is bankable but the buyer is not, the odds of getting the deal financed are modest at best.

Owner Financing

In consulting with a wide array of business owners, almost all unequivocally say they will never finance the sale of their business. While I absolutely agree the best arrangement is usually to get all your cash, shake hands, and run out the door, the reality is today's economic climate may require some element of owner financing in a majority of business sales. Both buyers and lenders are beginning to look to the seller to take back some paper in the deal.

Remember, when financing part of the deal where the remaining portion is financed by a bank, the seller note will be unsecured. Owner financing has risks—no question. You do not want to be forced to take back your own company a few years down the road because the buyer failed to make necessary payments to you and, in the meantime, has trashed your once productive business. It becomes necessary, therefore, to sell to the right buyer. As presented in the previous chapter, terms dictate the price, so make absolutely sure your terms have been properly vetted and then stick to them. Remember, the only thing worse than not getting the price you want is not getting the price you need.

Conditional Performance Notes

Simply stated, this type of note is based on the business performing financially to a predetermined base number, called a "benchmark," to pay the note. For example, if the gross profit reaches the "benchmark" in each quarter after the sale, the seller gets his note payment. The seller gets a percentage payment based on the level of the benchmark amount attained in that quarter.

An earn-out note is actually a "bridge" financing structure between what the buyer is willing to pay and what the seller requires for a sale price. It is a guarantee to the buyer that he will not have to pay for the earn-out amount until the business has performed over a certain period of time. Earn-out notes are common in merger and acquisition deals and are a way to bridge the gap between the parties.

Down Payments

Sellers want as much as they can get at closing, and buyers, regardless of their financial strength, usually want as much "leverage" as they can get in the transaction. The old adage of using other people's money comes into play in determining the amount of the down payment. Even if a buyer is very well financed, or the acquiring company is much larger than the target acquisition, "the least amount down" is typically the buyer's mantra.

If most sellers had their way, every deal would be all cash at closing. All cash deals are done on occasion, but a general rule is the structure for an all cash deal comes at a significant discount over the same deal with payment terms.

In addition, pledged security for future note payments is usually not available nor is it typical. The lending bank will be in a first security position after closing, automatically putting the seller in second position. As such, the general rule of thumb in a business acquisition is that the business being purchased has to stand on its own to fund or "make" the deal.

Deal structure plays a key role in almost every business sale. And so it is important business owners become familiar with financing options and be flexible to fit them into their financial picture in order to sell their company.

Listen and Learn

There is the anecdotal argument that there are potentially more buyers out there than ever before; corporate layoffs and cutbacks have thrown a lot of Americans out of work and a great many of them are looking for ways to get back on the horse.

Unemployment, stock market volatility, and historic low interest rates should mean that a new wave of business buyers are looking to buy a thriving business. We also have an aging population and fewer deals being done…that should also mean motivated sellers. The two together should spell good news for anyone who wants to sell.

So then why do only 30% of small companies get sold? True, finance does play its part, but by far the biggest problem is the inflexible seller and unrealistic buyer. If you believe there are lots of cash buyers out there, I'm sorry to say it, but you're dreaming. Likewise, buyers who think they can buy a solid company for no money down are also fantasizing.

As a seller, you can play your part by recognizing that buying a business today is price-sensitive; price your company too high, and you won't even get a look. So consider your business, the industry, similar businesses around you, the economy, AND the marketplace when it comes to selling. Simply listen to what the buyer hopes to achieve by buying your company and set your terms accordingly. The price takes care of itself if the buyer and the seller are motivated.

For now though, take a moment to consider the words of one of the country's leading corporate buyers, Warren Buffett:

"Price Is What You Pay, Value Is What You Get."

The Art of the Exit: Get What You Need—and It's Not Always Dollars

Let's take a moment to recalibrate.

The market is littered with business books that discuss the likely nuances of selling a business. From the business valuation process and how you should present your company for sale to the development of strategies on formulating the sales support team, you need to market your business if you want to get top dollar and the business book shelves have it covered. These are all important because as you can see, there is both an art and science when selling your business.

But *The Exit Equation* takes a fundamentally different approach as to where the process should start, how it should be vetted, and what the components of the plan should consider. *The Exit Equation* starts with the end in mind and works the process backwards. Now this may seem a little unorthodox at first glance, but we can't go about creating a plan if we do not know how we will gauge success.

As we presented back in Chapter 3, a good plan is born from knowing yourself and your company. If you are going to bridge the gap between operating your company now and successfully leaving it at a time of your choosing, you're going to need some introspection.

Many business owners are Type A personalities, driven by intuition, invention, and investment. They are not afraid to rely on themselves, and they will kick your ass if you get in the way. In a strange kind of way, they tend to be doers more than they are thinkers. Their lack of planning is often made up with excruciating effort and perseverance. Their impatience is no virtue. It is because of this mentality that business owners stumble more than they should and genuinely believe that leaving their company requires more action than planning. This is simply not true.

Many business owners believe that selling their business results in having the money and time to do the things they have always dreamed of doing. This prospect is certainly exciting; however, the loss of purpose and social connections that come with being a former business owner often leave the exited owner feeling unfulfilled and empty. If you do not believe me, talk to a few retirees and ask them what their biggest surprise was when they left. More often than not, it was the challenge of filling the hole. What to do with their time and how to engage themselves into something with purpose is at the core of their retirement day frustrations.

For most business owners, selling their business is a real game-changer. Far too many focus almost exclusively on the money, and when they do, there is still a component of their lives missing. This is why we consistently challenge you to think more about the the hole that needs to be filled once you leave your company and what you want to do to fill it. It is from this perspective that we start to strategize an exit strategy that actually works.

To make matters even cloudier, when you factor in the loss of salary and the reality of having to pay for some of the perks and daily expenses the company used to pay for you, business owners begin to understand the intricacies of the exit equation. This is the fundamental reason why, before you put the FOR SALE sign in the front window, we encourage you to take stock in the value of strategizing and planning.

At this juncture of the book we have spent some time on starting at the end and working the process backwards. We have discussed coming to an understanding as to why you want to sell your business and the timeframe for your departure. We then reviewed the basis for an exit plan and laid out how to go about accumulating the information and mindset necessary to plan your exit. Chapters 4, 5, and 6 provided the insights necessary to begin to prepare the company for your exit, while Chapters 7 and 8 reviewed the issues you will likely need to address in your preparation to negotiate your departure.

This chapter reaffirms the intrinsic reasons for your exit because these, much like your decision to depart, must be thoroughly vetted if you want to achieve the dream without regret for having done it the wrong way.

The Pendulum Swings

If you are like a majority of business owners, especially those who have owned their businesses for a long period of time, you have gone through a transition that starts with your business depending on you and concluding with you depending on your business.

An example of this transitional evolution centers on the transfer of cash. In the early days, your business needed you because it needed cash. We all know that cash is king and without it your business will surely die. But in those early days the cash your business needed wasn't just what you put into it, it also included the cash you did not take out of it. If you have been a business owner for a long time, you understood early in the great game of business that your cash needed to remain in the business if you were to have any chance of surviving, let alone grow. Your business needed you and your cash.

Now you find yourself on the tail end of the journey and now the pendulum has swung completely to the other side. You have come to rely on your business more than ever. Your lifestyle is an extension of your business, and now, after years of feeding your money to the business to keep it strong and growing, you find yourself taking money out of the business. Whether it's the result of a higher than market wage, numerous "business" trips that double as vacations, hefty bonuses, a new car and corporate gas card, or a bottomless expense account, your business is now paying you for your sweat equity and risk-taking. Although you can easily justify these expenses, the fact is you have been systematically spending the money that should only come from the sale of your business. You see, much of the money you have spent, if left in the company, would have created a magnificent company endeared to many buyers. Instead, you have slowly drained many of the growing assets of your business and now you find yourself ready to depart and thinking of a glorious payday.

This scenario is not atypical of the average, long-tenured business owner who has benefitted from a successful business. It seems many business owners are rather quick to compensate themselves for their hard work, and perhaps rightly so, to a degree. When a business is successful it generates profits, and if done correctly, those profits turn to cash (recall my earlier comments that it is far better to be profitable in paper than to be profitable on paper). The generated cash can then be used for a variety of purposes. Increased salaries and/or fringe benefits, investments in new expertise, updated technology, new equipment, research and development, rainy day fund, and/or bonuses are just examples of how cash is either invested in the company or spent outside the company. When invested or expended in moderation, the company can continue down the path toward long-term profitability; when spent too fast or not in the right areas, the company suffers. These results are apparent when you consider the economic downturn of 2008 and how many good companies, whose owners lived high on the hog and expended too much money on things not benefitting the company, started to suffer and ultimately fail.

Although you have every right to take from your company what you want, it is important you understand what your company needs. After all, in many instances your nest egg is tied to the equity in your company. What you are spending today as the owner of the business is, in many ways, proportional to what you won't get when you sell the company. Haphazardly spending your equity is no different than haphazardly spending your retirement funds. At some point you will begin to realize that it all comes from the same pot!

Now, let's look at this scenario from the opposite perspective. What do you need from your company? No doubt, your immediate thoughts turned to cash. Yes, cash is great, but how much is enough? Is cash the only thing your company can give you? My argument is that at some point your company must give you something more; perhaps it's an intangible that cannot be counted or stacked. As you give solace to the idea that it just may be time to sell the business and get on with living outside the fishbowl of your company, your expectations should begin to focus on quality not quantity. The stress of finding sales, the challenges of making payroll, and the frustrations of sorting through problems and failed expectations take a toll. These issues beat you down; you have trouble sleeping; your health suffers; your relationships with those around you are strained. For what? Because you need cash, or is it that you want more cash? At what point does it become more about quality of life over quantity of life? Planning for your post-company-owner days has to begin at some point, and when it does, my suggestion is that you start with the end in mind and prepare to implement a strategy that gets you what you need, not what you think you want.

Ask Yourself the Tough Questions

A few years ago, I sold one of my businesses. It was challenging in terms of leaving a company I had built from scratch, not knowing what the future might have in store for me, and walking away from the money and freedom that comes from owning a successful business. It was in 2006-2007. There were thunderheads on the horizon, and I felt something was up. My staff had been with me a long time, and I sensed they were growing restless. You see, I ran a consulting company and my greatest assets got up and walked out the office door each day at 5 p.m. I had been in this type of business for many years, so my concern always centered on whether those assets would come back the next day.

With external and internal factors tugging at me, I began the process of preparing myself and my company for my departure. I set out to complete this challenging chain of events using the strategies and tactics laid out in this book. I began to ask myself what was important to me and my family.

I self-evaluated where I was in my life and what I still wanted to do. I recalled the stresses and challenges of building the company and dealing with the demands of clients and my employees. I had built a reasonable nest egg for myself and knew there was more out there for me. Most importantly, I was not going to work harder for less. The ground swell of economic concerns became deafening. The results were felt by my company in terms of difficulties obtaining new contracts and getting paid for the ones we already had. Some of my key staff had decided to move on and some of the key staff that remained were simply riding along, enjoying the view. I had legitimate reasons to worry.

I embarked on a multi-path strategy to evaluate all my options. I was fortunate, if not wise, because I had reinvested in the company and had maintained operating parameters that were quite reasonable. I was bankable, and the company was ready for me to depart. My first option was to privately solicit a few firms that might have an interest in acquiring my company. I did this discreetly through my attorney whose office was located in a major metro market (unlike most of my offices). I also pursued a strategy of self-financing my departure through the excess cash flow generated by the company, for which I was the majority shareholder. In addition, I quietly pursued a sales option with my primary senior staffers who I had had numerous conversations with over the years regarding my departure at some point in time in the future.

Each strategy had its own set of tactics, and I pursued all of them concurrently. As suspected, the economic downturn occurred in 2008, but I was prepared. I sold and closed the deal on January 1, 2009—an internal cash deal, no seller financing, no performance agreement. All of this happened because I asked myself the important questions and went about a strategy of preparing me and my company for my departure.

Procrastination Is the Enemy

Most business owners hesitate when it comes to making decisions about exiting their business. Why? Because in many instances the business is the only thing they know. Their life is bound by the intricacies of their business and their fear of what the future might be without the company. This is a prevalent mindset of business owners. They have too much to give up, and they find any and every excuse imaginable to delay their exit planning. It does not matter what industry they are in or their age. There seems to be no correlation between their health, the structure of their company, or the thickness of their wallet. What's most disturbing is that if you sit down and chat with them, often the conversation turns toward their desire to exit their companies. They talk of the stress and the frustrations. They lament the tactics of competition and the intrusion of government. For many, they simply get to the point where they do not have the stamina, or even in many ways the desire, to keep their foot on the gas pedal. But at the end of the day, despite all their complaining, they cannot or will not pull the trigger and begin the process of preparing themselves and their company for their departure.

I have had the frustrating honor to work with a baby boomer-aged business owner who falls squarely into this trap. He:

- Owns a 30-year-old business and is very good at what he does;

- Keeps his hand in the local and state process that regulates his business;
- Is intricately involved in a trade group of his peers from around the country who share their individual challenges and successes so each can learn from the other;
- Studies his market and its opportunities and works with the very best local, regional, and national consultants and engineers to design and create functional and economically viable projects;
- Has been successful and has learned to force himself to develop strategic plans and complement those plans with annual budgets;
- Invests in talent and technology and is not afraid to try something new; and
- Is also increasingly frustrated with his company, the politics and economy of the region, and the challenges of driving the business each and every day.

When confronted with the obviousness of his situation, he is quick to mention his desire to take his equity and go. But when you dig a little deeper and get him to retrospectively consider his situation and what he really wants to do, you find that all he really wants is to do less baby-sitting. You see, in this instance, he is his company, and he has surrounded himself with a staff that is quite talented but has come to rely on him. He is the leader; he makes the decisions. As he often puts it, no one on his staff wants to get out of the backseat and drive the car; they are all content to sit there and enjoy the ride. If he had his druthers, he loves doing what he does, but he just does not like having to drag everyone else along. So it was with this backdrop that we sat down to etch out an exit strategy that allowed him to continue to do what he loves but with less baggage.

The subsequent conversations were lively, thought-provoking, and on the mark. We:

- Developed multiple scenarios that accomplished the objective and gave him what he wanted;
- Sorted through the tax considerations and the personnel limitations;
- Accounted for the financial impact and mitigated the obvious risks; and
- Worked through the marketing issues and the operational considerations of the transition.

In the end, the exit plan was practical, logical, and doable. Was there risk? Of course there was. What deal does not have some element of inherent risk? But in the end he relented and decided to sit tight. Despite his increasing frustrations and attempts to design and implement an exit strategy on his own that imploded time and time again, the new plan was nixed because he was not ready to go. Although he lamented many things about his own company, in the end he was not ready to let go of the steering wheel.

This scenario is not surprising when you really get into the details with many business owners. Admittedly, it is a big decision to leave your company and do something else. It may take you a while to be prepared for it, emotionally and psychologically. You may also be so busy dealing with the day to day that you repeatedly put long-term issues on the backburner.

Some hesitation is perfectly normal; procrastination, however, could cost you dearly. The art of the exit is to know what you want to gain from the sale of your business and to go for it; it's not to sit around stalling. The art of exiting a business is also to sell when you *want* to sell and not to leave it so late that you *have* to sell.

Starting a business is always easier than getting out of one. Planning your exit not only means you are less likely to leave money on the table, but you'll be more likely to gain the terms and conditions you need from your sale to walk into the next stage of your life completely unencumbered.

There's a saying that sums it all up: ***failing to plan is planning to fail.***

It's probably time to put yourself first on the list and begin the planning process. If planned correctly, you will not regret it and will only kick yourself in the ass for not having done it earlier. Those who do regret selling out are typically the ones who short-change themselves and go about it in a way that is poorly conceived, poorly planned, and poorly executed.

I said this in the Prologue, and it is worth noting again: real wealth is not made simply by starting a company, and it's not made simply by growing your company. Real wealth is made by selling your company.

An Internal Sale: The Golden Rules

Chief lieutenants always make great successors. Your son could certainly do the job. Your management team has always had your back, and they know exactly what you want done. Your most tenured employee really wants to have a chance to run the shop, and hell, he's earned it.

An internal sale is often the most attractive option for a small business owner, and in its own unique way, it's the easiest way to get out. Selling to family, managers, or key employees helps the business continue as is and provides employment for the people who have helped you along the way.

Selling to an internal candidate also aids any need you have to protect your legacy. In fact, not having to find a buyer and being able to train and transition your business to an internal successor who already knows the company is very attractive. There's something very rewarding about the idea of passing on your pride and joy to someone who presumably cares about it just as much as you do.

But before you chase the obvious and take the short cut to exiting your company, beware of the seemingly innocuous tripping hazards along the way. You've become emotionally invested in your company; it's tempting to want to pass it on to someone you personally have trained, another true believer, someone in the company or family who will preserve your legacy. That's what many business owners are looking for. The fictional Willy Wonka summed it up when he concocted an incredible challenge to find the most devoted Wonka customer, all so he could hand his chocolate empire to the little boy who cared just as much about his product as he did.

Of course, you don't need to go to quite those lengths, but it's easy to see why the thought is so appealing. Handing over the reins to an internal successor is not as easy as it would appear. The presumption is there is less due diligence needed and any successor you have trained will operate the company the same way you have. These apparent benefits to an internal sale are superficial at best.

Internal successors still pose a risk. There is always that legitimate concern that your handpicked successor may not be as much of a risk-taker as you have been. Another critical issue is he or she may not be as bankable as you might think. And finally, you are not as likely to negotiate in a manner that best represents your truest self-interests, and this is a fundamental mistake. In fact, you may even be willing to finance the deal because you mistakenly believe your successor simply cannot fail. These are real threats to your departure and your wallet.

As tempting as it can be to want to see your son, daughter, nephew, or another family member toiling away at the family business or as philanthropic as it may seem to sell the company to an employee who started his business life working for you as an intern, you need to look at the prospect very carefully.

Be dispassionate about the potential successors in your business—ask yourself if they can really do the job. Do not be swayed by family or other loyalties. Likewise, consider the finances; can an internal succession work for you financially? Will it give you the liquidity you need for the next stage of your life?

It's often the case that employees and second-generation family don't have the means to pay cash for the business and may well look to the business itself to fund the purchase. Would that work for you? If you need a considerable lump sum up front, probably not; this may be a recipe for disaster.

If you're honest with yourself and perform your commensurate due diligence, if you find there is no worthy successor within the family or the company, you will need to look for an external buyer for your company.

It's my strong recommendation that if you think you have an internal candidate, don't put all your eggs into just the one basket. Always consider both internal and external succession options; that way if one option does not materialize or one is far more attractive to you than the other, you can rest easy knowing you did it right. Remember what we talked about at the beginning of this book; in many instances this may be the first time you will ever sell a business, and there is plenty you might not be privy to in consideration of your limited experience. It is imperative you do it right, and you do it right the first time; there are no do-overs.

For purposes of exploring the issues at hand when considering an internal sale, let's review the options and their corresponding challenges.

Option 1: Family Succession

Many business owners love the idea of passing their business on to family. They picture working side by side with their offspring for the good of their business or feel satisfied just knowing the company they lovingly created is in the hands of the next generation.

But you should be conscious of the problems you may create by simply entering into a discussion about this type of succession planning. Before you even broach the subject, you need to objectively assess the strength of your family and your implied successor. For instance, is the family functional, and does it respect the need for a commitment to the chain-of-command? You do not want to make a delicate or dysfunctional family any worse by putting extra pressure on it. Moreover, if the family has grown to expect all that you have provided, and it cannot seem to relate risk with return, then this option may not work.

Family succession planning can be extra complicated; the relationships involved, the emotions, the internal politics, perceived favoritism…all can rip a family apart if succession isn't handled well. Will your kids fight for decades over perceived slights when transferring your business, for instance, especially if one of them seems to walk away with everything?

There is a reason why 70% of family-owned businesses never survive the transition from founder to the next generation. It is a staggering statistic, but it is the result of family discord and lack of a common vision for the company that are the most common reasons cited for transitional failure (alongside taxes). Likewise, poor training can also be a problem (the new owner may be a "chip off the old block" but that does not mean he or she will do it as well as you have).

It does not help if the founder or former owner never really handed over de-facto control. This is a common mistake business owners make when internally transitioning their business. When you cannot resist the temptation to step in when things get tough, succession to a family member is tantamount to treason. It is easier to interfere when it's your children who are now running the business as opposed to a non-family person.

Then there's the rightful gift mentality. This is when a family member who has worked diligently by your side expects the business to come their way when you are done. This is a common perception and one you may have promulgated by not having a truthful discussion a few years ago as to your intentions. People who are just gifted a company as opposed to buying it (if that's the route you choose to go down) just don't have the same motivation if it all comes to them too easily. Almost everyone who works and earns their share always has a keener and deeper appreciation for having earned it. For that singular reason, I always recommend selling the business even to your family members in some form.

If you're considering handing your business over to a family member, make sure you objectively consider the business, the business process, customary business transactions, the ability of the successor, and the perception of the successor in the eyes of your customers, clients, vendors, suppliers, and employees. If you think family succession is for you, I can almost guarantee you that you are too close to the situation, and it will be imperative for you to retain outside counsel to objectively pursue your wishes. Successful succession planning takes time, a commitment to your needs, and a steadfast hand in making transitional decisions that align the sale (or transition) of the business with your needs.

Here we come back to the key point of any succession, family or otherwise. You need to make sure you're well looked after once the next generation—family or key employee—takes over. You're not going to want to leave your company voluntarily if you're worried that your financial security is not assured. That's a huge obstacle to genuine family succession and often another reason the outgoing owner is reluctant to hand over de facto control, which in turn can lead to the failure of a second generation family business.

So you need to choose the right person to take over as owner and you need to do it in a manner that best assures success.

There's an old adage, which may apply here. It is often said Grandpa establishes the business; Dad grows the business; and Junior loses the business. Family succession may appear the easiest, but it has unique challenges other exit strategies do not. Remain the businessman during this process; do not succumb to the challenges of being Mom or Dad.

Fair Doesn't Necessarily Mean Equal

The question of who gets what and how you can be fair to all of your children is often the biggest stumbling block in family succession. Small business owners often rack their brains to come up with innovative ways of sharing the company among offspring, only to find that the company suffers as siblings fight for control.

The important thing to remember here is that fair does not have to mean equal. You *don't* have to give your children equal ownership of the company. If your son has been working in the company for years, for instance, and is your natural successor, you may want to give him majority ownership in the company; in contrast, your daughter, who has never shown any aptitude or interest in the family business so far, may get an equity stake, or may get something else entirely.

It may not be equal, *but* judging by past events and ability, it is fair. Your son has contributed to the development of the company so far, whereas your daughter has not.

You may find that genuine equalization—where all offspring are treated exactly the same—just isn't possible. It sounds great in concept, but in reality, a company needs someone, preferably one person, to step up to the plate. It doesn't need equal owners at loggerheads because they can't agree on the way forward or siblings playing power games as they try to claw their way to the top or to a bigger payday.

Here's an important ideology to understand that may help you to address the problem: management and ownership are not the same. Just because someone has ownership in the company does not mean they have to manage it. You can, and often times should, split the two up.

You could, for instance, give your son and daughter equal ownership of the company, *but* appoint your son to manage and run it. You could transfer management to just one of your children but give all of them an equal amount of equity. Or it may be fairer to transfer a larger share of business ownership to the successor who is running the business and a smaller amount to those family members who are not involved in the day to day operations. Looking at it dispassionately, it may even be best to transfer ownership AND management to one family member, your chosen successor, and make completely different financial arrangements for your other children.

The choice certainly is yours, but just be sure to do what is best for the company—and your own financial well-being down the line.

It may be that there simply isn't enough of the pie to go around or to share; in which case, you're going to need to set expectations with your children beforehand. In extreme cases, you may just have to say "that's the way it is."

Try to find a workable solution, but don't dance around the issue forever; parents trying to be equal to all involved can, and have, stalled the succession planning process. The fact is that you need to put your business hat on and not think like a family man (or woman). Your business cannot be run by a committee of heirs, so put the company first.

Remember, It's Business Not Family

Choosing a successor, establishing a transitional timeline, and negotiating the deal can be fraught with emotional issues. The only thing you can do is to think of the business, first and foremost. Look at your potential successors and be objective; consider them as you would if you were hiring for the position from outside. Do they have the talent, skills, ambition, and passion you want to see from an outside manager? Do they have the ability to lead, and can they successfully make your employees want to follow them? The notion of leadership is crucial to the continued well-being of your company. Employees may find it difficult that you are leaving, but they may find it more difficult to follow Junior. Companies are not managed to success; they are led to success. It is imperative that, should you choose to follow this option, you are sure to devise a strategy and corresponding tactics that ensure a defining, beneficial, and logical succession.

This can be accomplished by linking succession planning to your business strategy. Choose a suitable successor based on what you want the company to achieve in the future. If your business is expanding overseas, for instance, choose the successor that will best lead that charge. If your heir apparent currently does not have these abilities, then take the time to educate and train him provided they have the aptitude for it. This notion goes back to the issue of your time horizon. Both you and your company need to be prepared for your departure. This may require a series of assignments, special initiatives, investments, and restructure. Make sure if this is the succession option you want, that you and Junior go about it the right way.

Remember, there are no do-overs.

Option 2: Management Team Succession

The good thing about a management succession is that it avoids the risk of relying on one single chosen successor.

Another bonus of selling to management is their familiarity with the business and their inherent self-interests. They already know the business, they are keen on the intricacies of your daily operations and long-term strategies, and they are a known commodity to your employees at large.

As the new owners, they will bring a sense of renewed energy to the company, and they will be eager to implement some or all of the often discussed initiatives you may never have been in favor of or simply did not have the ambition or risk-tolerance to implement. Indeed, we often find that a newly sold company enjoys dramatic growth after a buyout; that's usually because talented and skilled managers have more incentive and control than they ever had before.

If your future financial health depends on the success of the company, leaving it in the hands of your top performing employees or proven managers can give you the assurance you need to step away and enjoy the next phase of your life unhindered.

But just picking someone is not the answer to the differential equation that is a successful exit strategy. One of the critical issues that come into play under this option is that of bankability. Do all members of the acquiring management team have the ability to invest capital into the sale? If not, how does the ownership interest of each member of the team shake out? Just like the challenges of a family succession, selling to your management team can present an ownership/management quandary. How does everyone participate when some cannot generate the cash needed to close the deal?

In these instances, you may need to finance some upfront capital to make the deal work. Selling to your management team could also prove to be one of the very best options for you. Depending on the terms you negotiate, you could retain a commensurate stake in the business and maintain control until all the debt financing is repaid. In between, you reduce your hours and perhaps only focus on those areas of the business that truly interest you, while the owner-managers run the rest. This sort of tiered exit strategy could work well for both parties.

There is need for a word of caution at this juncture of the discussion. Your management team may work really well under your tutelage, but they may struggle to find themselves and their collective ability if you are not the steady driving force behind them. Do not underestimate this challenge. It is always different sitting in the big chair. Everyone thinks they can do it; managing from a position of power and leverage always seems easy to the adolescent manager. Truth be told, directing a company is no small matter. You are all too keen on the challenges of getting good people, especially those who are high achievers, to work together. It seems as though everyone can and wants to skin the cat their own way. To them it's easy. But in reality, making payroll is not what it appears.

Take the time needed to have candid discussions with your team. Tell them how you feel and what you find to be your most challenging issues as the owner of the company. Allow them to ask questions and instill a sense of true camaraderie amongst all. Hold these discussions routinely as you contemplate your transition from the company. Similar to our discussion earlier in the book, find out what they want to accomplish individually. Find out why they want to have an equity stake. Make sure they understand the risks and the collateral needed to be an owner. In the end, some members of your team may be great managers but poor owners. Be objective and listen. Do your due diligence and then decide what is best for you and your company. Remember, these types of discussions can be both beneficial and detrimental. If one of your managers cannot or will not assume the risk of the group, they may feel unwelcomed and leave your company. Likewise, if the other members of the team are willing to do what is needed but one member is an outlier, the trust and confidence of the group may be challenged. Inasmuch as management teams can be logical successors, the mere process of negotiations can cloud the line between ownership and management.

On the positive side, a management buyout may allow you to ask for a higher price; assuming you can avoid feeling loyal to the people across the table, selling to management plays to your advantage. Inevitably, these folks know the true potential of the company, and they have probably had to throttle back their abilities and ambitions while you were at the helm. Why? Because as we have discussed previously, long-tenured business owners tend to become risk-averse as they get older, and they have a strong tendency to not drive the business as hard as they did when they were younger. Moreover, as the business owner, you probably diverted more money from the company than you should have these last few years, and now with you out of the way, the management team can get down to making some real money.

Similarly, to my recommendation involving pursuit of multiple options when considering a family succession, it is not unusual for owners to offer the company to management while also considering outside buyers. Although you may disagree with my next assertion, if you decide to pursue multiple options concurrently, do not make your intentions known. You will do yourself a complete disservice if you only pursue one option. Also, it is logical for your management team to feel betrayed if you tell them you love them but you are pursuing other options as you negotiate with them. In my opinion, they simply do not need to know what your strategies and tactics are because in the end you must defend yourself above all else.

Remember what we said at the outset of this book—an effective exit strategy must be based on you recognizing what is important to you in the next phase of your life, and you must diligently defend what you need and under what terms. You must avert your common historical process of putting your employees ahead of yourself. There is nothing wrong with being professionally ruthless to get what you deserve and need.

Option 3: Selling to a Key Employee

Of all the internal options presented, this one has some great advantages.

Successful transitioning, whether you are talking about a sports team which changes coaches, the election of a new president, or the sale of a business, relies on a few fundamental principles: the scope of the message, consistency of purpose, reliability of action, and the ability to follow through.

Internal business sales have a few distinct benefits over their external business sale counterparts. When you consider the scope and application of each of the aforementioned transition issues, internal sales are usually strongly supported by the notions of the scope of the message and the consistency of purpose. I would argue that reliability of action and the ability to follow through are better addressed through an outside sale. Let's focus briefly on the first two issues.

When you consider a transition to a new business owner and that new owner is someone internal to the organization (e.g., family successor, your management team, or a key employee), the scope of the message resonates with your staff. Because the new owner is a trusted member of the staff, the scope of the business is likely to remain reasonably consistent. I say reasonably because some change is inevitable. Issues beyond the control of the new owner, even if the new owner is selected from the inside, will require change at some point. But in the short term, everyone on the staff will expect continued clarity in the scope of the message.

In addition, because the new owner is an inside guy/gal, there is an expected consistency of purpose within the company. Certainly, the new owner has every right to change the direction and application of the company, but these types of ideological changes generally come about slowly. New owners, much like new spouses, tend to ease into the new relationship, often masking what they really want to do or say in support of the best interests of the team. Eventually, however, these opinions and desires find their way to daylight and changes are made.

So how do these two fundamental issues play out in an internal sale, and why does the key employee option often prove to be effective? It boils down to politics, committee ineptitude, and the power of one.

When talking about the scope of the message and the consistency of purpose, internal politics usually undermine the family successor process. For many employees, the fact Junior has taken over the company is more a result of politics than it is of purposefulness. For most, if Junior hasn't earned it, Junior shouldn't get it. Add to this philosophical demeanor the notion that you, the former owner, desperately want to see Junior succeed, and you may be too trigger happy to come in and save the day if junior is in trouble. Politics inherent to the family succession option are tough to overcome.

As far as the sale of your company to your management team, it sounds good on paper but has trouble in practicality. In most instances, this group is comprised of high-performing people who believe in themselves and their decisions. Management by committee is wrought with too much internal strife, backstabbing, and one-upmanship. Although the group may reach consensus in the boardroom, it rarely finds its way onto the shop floor.

This leaves us with the lone key employee. As a single leader, there is zero concern over politics because no one needs an excuse or an alibi. In similar fashion, the need to find consensus when making decisions simply does not exist when the business is led by one person.

As for you, they business seller, you can now focus your efforts toward the promulgation of a sale in a one-on-one negotiation. No multi-personalities or hidden agendas. When you add these realities to your assessment of the risk-tolerance and bankability of your would-be buyer, you now have a recipe for a productive negotiation that gives you the best opportunity to reach a deal on your terms.

The View From the Big Chair

Once you decide to pursue an internal sale to a key employee, there are various things you can do to give them the very best chance of success once you've handed over the reins. Do not skimp on this part; it could mean the difference between your company thriving and surviving after you're gone or going down the tubes and taking your money (or at least some of it if you financed the deal) with it.

All of these things demonstrate how important it is to begin your exit planning early.

Training

Life in the big chair is different, so no matter how good your successor might be, they have to get used to sitting in the chair.

The biggest reason many businesses fail after an internal succession is a lack of training. If you're planning to sell or hand over to a family member, make sure they know the ropes beforehand. This is where your time horizon comes into play.

You may not think it, but even if you're planning a management succession, training is still important too. Chances are you personally have current responsibilities your management team doesn't; perhaps you take care of all client and customer liaison while they deal more with the day-to-day running of the business, for instance.

You're going to want to train them and introduce them to key clients or customers before you leave. Take advantage of the time you have and move managers around; ensure they have significant experience of all areas of the business, and help them develop key relationships with suppliers, contacts, clients, or customers that you have developed over the years.

Arm them with the knowledge and confidence they need to do the job and company justice.

Make Sure They Earn It

This is especially true in family succession. Parachuting your son or daughter into position without any prior experience is only going to cause frustration and resentment among your employees. You need your successor to be respected and able to lead the company.

Your children may have the right to inherit the business, but that does not mean they have an automatic right to manage it. Demonstrate to them and to your employees that they must be accountable; just like any other employee, they must perform. You may want to make it clear that they will not automatically assume leadership after succession or transition if they haven't proved they deserve it on merit. Make them work for the role; they will become better owners and managers because of it.

Tidy Up

As part of the succession planning, you need to clarify any informal arrangements you have within the company. These arrangements may not work for the new owner, for instance; it's also unfair to saddle a new owner, whether management or family, with informal agreements they know nothing about or didn't agree to in the first place.

So spend this time formalizing any arrangements and clarifying important positions, such as which assets belong to you personally and which belong to the business. You would need to do it for an external sale, so don't shirk the responsibility when planning an internal succession.

Set a Date and Stick to It

You may find a graduated retirement works best for an internal sale, but it's still important to pick a date and stick to it. Consider carefully how you will slowly hand over control during the succession, and make sure you have a planned end-date.

A good rule of thumb as the succession approaches is to take longer absences away from the company; not only is it important for the new boss, employees, customers, and suppliers alike to get used to the idea that you are not there, it's also useful for you to start experiencing life after selling the business.

> **SPECIAL CONSIDERATIONS:** *Understand the New Generation Will Do Things Differently*

Much as we are different from our parents, the next generation is even more drastically removed from our line of thinking. They have different ambitions and work habits, are more technologically savvy, and in general, have experienced a much easier life than we did. I'm not whining about it, but we Baby Boomers have been so instrumental in changing the face of the United States that we have literally changed life for those who came after us.

Give them the ball and let them run with it. If they want to introduce more family-friendly workspaces, or flexible work hours, or allow staff to work from home occasionally for instance, so be it. If they decide a larger corporate investment is needed in computer information technology, don't preempt them from making and implementing the decision. If they decide to compete differently than you did, what's to say they are not right? Don't chant about how it was different in your day.

Recognize that whoever takes over from you, even if they have been trained by you, will do things differently. It's just human nature. As long as what they do works for the firm (and you need to give them a chance to find that out), it's all good.

Accept Your New Role

On that note, you're going to have to learn how to accept your new role, whatever it may be. If you've promised to walk away into the sunset and simply take the payment checks, then make sure you do so and don't keep "popping in" to interfere. Remember, you have to give de facto command to your successor or your company will never survive the succession.

Your successor will never earn the respect and command of your lifetime suppliers, customers and loyal employees if you're always there in the background, just "checking to see if everything is okay" or having informal little state of the company meetings with employees by the water cooler.

If you do want an ongoing role within the company, make sure you define it succinctly, and know your new responsibilities, authority, and accountability…and don't step over the line. Be disciplined; if employees still come to you with problems that should be handled by the new owner (and they will—employees often fear change), send them away. Stick to your new role and soon everyone will learn what you are—and are not—there for.

An internal succession can be the easiest and a rewarding choice when it comes to transitioning your business *if* you handle it well. Take emotion out of it and judge objectively, but don't be afraid to admit that an internal succession just isn't in the cards either if you don't have a worthy successor. If that is the case, you're going to need to look to an external sale.

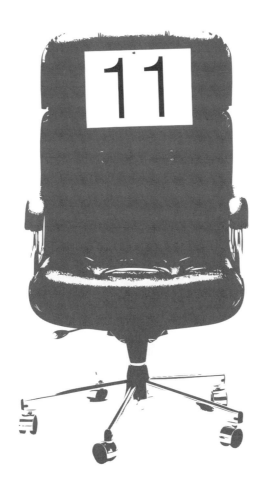

An External Sale

If you've decided an internal sale isn't for you, you're going to have to think about which form of external succession works best. You could sell the stock and therefore ownership of the business to an outside buyer or simply sell select assets the company owns. Traditionally, tax and liability considerations mean that sellers usually prefer stock sales, while buyers prefer asset purchases. You need to decide which type of sale is doable and work with a potential buyer to make sure you're both happy at the end of the day.

There are many reasons why you may opt for an external sale, and it isn't just because you lack an authentic internal successor. You are more likely to be able to sell the business for its true value, for instance, if you sell it externally, with less personal implications for you and your staff.

Likewise, you reduce the risk of key employees jumping ship if you go straight for an external sale. Why? Because if you try for an internal sale with your managers or key employees and it falls through, those same people may well have a natural reluctance to stay at the firm afterwards. And as an added bonus to an external sale, there's less chance of a breach of confidentiality as the least number of people that know about the potential sale, the better.

The question now, of course, is how do you find a willing buyer?

Come Out, Come Out Wherever You Are

In the famous words of Stephen Covey: first things first. Let me say that identifying potential buyers is always going to be easier if you've analyzed your business and understand the reasons for a sale, as well as knowing what you want to receive from it. If you haven't done the latter yet, go back to what has been suggested throughout this book and do the work recommended.

You are now going to base your research on the analysis you have already done of your company to draw up a list of likely buyers. This is an important first step in the process of finding a buyer. Your list should consider a number of options, including competitors, companies with ancillary businesses to yours, companies similar to yours but located in other geographic areas, and serial entrepreneurs. You should also include discussions with your attorney and accountant, as these professionals can serve as your representatives in the solicitation process. Let them know what you wish to do, and ask them to keep their eyes open to potential opportunities. You may also decide to seek out a business broker to aid in the search.

A word of caution in this regard—although these folks are generally good at what they do and they certainly have their own style and book of business to rely upon, make sure the confidentiality agreement you execute protects your interests. In addition, make sure the general asking price (which many brokers want to know in advance) is presented in a broad range and contingent upon the terms of the sale. My suggestion is that brokers be used to simply get the prospective buyer to the table; you should do your own negotiating (always with your attorney and accountant nearby).

The other issue that comes into play is the notion of "listing" the business for sale. You will find it far more appealing and protective of your company if you try to sell quietly rather than pronouncing to the world that you have had enough. I see too many businesses that hang the "For Sale" sign in the front window, and the owner always whines about the resultant string of inquiries and bargain hunters. The stronger the company looks, the better the opportunity to get what you need. Everyone should know the business is solid, and you are in it for the long haul (even if you are lying).

Once you have made the list, be sure to segregate it into the two groups we identified and discussed previously: value buyers and lifestyle buyers. Value buyers are those folks who are cost-driven, while lifestyle buyers tend to be premium buyers who are interested in your company because of the industry it is in, the customers you have, or the location of your company.

A one-off sale to an interested but previously unconnected buyer could happen, but it's much more likely that your business will be acquired by another company you have identified.

Acquisition in Detail

As you initiate the process of selling, your list of potential acquirers is the key starting point. Look for both potential horizontal and vertical acquirers. You might hate the idea of selling to a competitor—we're all fiercely protective of our territory—but you can't afford to be emotional about it. A competitor is often your best potential buyer because they know the industry and the market, and they hate the idea of competing against someone new.

In order to come up with the list of potential buyers, ask some key questions: who would benefit more from the business? Who is it worth the most to? Which competitors or businesses would find your company attractive to buy, perhaps because your products complement their own range or because they'd rather buy you than compete with you?

What potential synergies could you offer to buyers? Which businesses could benefit from sales-driven, cost-driven, or distribution-driven synergy with your company? If you merged or were acquired by that company, would the value and performance of both companies combined be greater than the separate entities?

Think cleverly and analyze your options carefully; identify any strengths and weaknesses of potential buyers and look for any areas where your business could add value. Do you have a great distribution system, for instance? If so, you might want to approach one of your potential acquirers that doesn't; they could potentially be interested in buying you for your distribution set-up alone.

Likewise, is there a gap in their business—maybe in its geographic coverage or in its product lines or market segment—that could be improved by buying your company?

Of course, a potential acquirer may not necessarily be a competitor; they could be in an unrelated industry or be a vertical acquirer (an acquisition in which the acquirer and the target company are in the same industry but focus on different parts of the industry or production process) as opposed to a horizontal acquirer (an acquisition by one company of another company in the same industry). Perhaps they would want your business to allow them to expand into a new market or offer a new product to existing customers? It could also be that the technology or a patent that you have at your disposal will allow them to leapfrog development and give them critical capabilities faster than they could develop them on their own.

Selling to a Competitor

Let's talk a little bit more about the potential to sell your business to a competitor. You may hate the idea (after all, you've probably spent most of your business life competing against them), but the fact remains that selling to a competitor could be the basis for a great deal.

I'm talking here of either a direct competitor (one that is competing with you side by side on price, service, product, or more), an indirect competitor (a company that maybe competes with you on some products as part of selling other products/services but rarely competes with a full line), or a near competitor (direct competitor but in a different territory).

A competitor may be willing to buy a competing business in order to increase market share; gain equipment, facilities, or assets; leverage a better supply chain; gain highly skilled employees; and/or enjoy a better return on investment.

The fact is that buying your company could open up a whole new avenue of growth for your competitor and one that they probably could not get alone (or not without much time, effort, and money expended). Your contacts alone could take their business to the next level, plus there is the potential to increase profits through economies-of-scale since you are both in the same market or industry. These issues, plus the fact they don't have to worry about another company buying their competitor and making inroads into their market share, are factors that could lead to a higher price for your business.

It stands to reason, therefore, that your competitor is probably more open to negotiation than any other external buyer. And if you can use your knowledge about them to leverage the deal, even better!

Be Warned

The problem with negotiating with competitors, of course, is that you don't want to give away all your proprietary information, and you do not want your potential sale to be used against you. Take your time, and do not approach them under the pretense of selling your business. Consider a strategy disguised as a general discussion about opportunities for both of you. Broach the subject simply as a means to explore future joint efforts; this way you protect your interests and the value of your company. If there are synergies between the two of you, you can begin to gauge the interest of your competitor and their capacity for risk and growth.

Be aware, too, of the competitors who don't intend to buy in the first place, but will fake it in order to learn as much as they can about your company, suppliers, customers, employees, strategies, and more. It does happen and probably more than you'd like to think.

You'd be a fool to take their interest on faith. Treat any interest by a competitor very carefully, even if you were the one to go to them. Ensure a comprehensive confidentiality agreement is drawn and signed, containing non-interference provisions to protect customers, suppliers, employees, and anything proprietary to your company.

Never provide customer or supplier lists, financial information, or employee details until a Purchase Agreement is in place and you are confident the buyer is sincere. Then you can allow due diligence, but again, keep this firmly under control and on a short leash.

You should be asking them some pretty straightforward questions as soon as they show interest in your company. Questions like: why are they interested in the business, what are their long-term plans, how does your business fit in, do they need you in the picture, how will they finance the combined entity, what is the ability of their management team, how will the competitor merge the two corporate ideologies? But these are not all. Remember what we presented earlier in the book; find out how they intend to pay for the transaction, what role you might need to play, where they bank, and if they are bankable. Ask and then listen.

Whether you are talking to a competitor or any other potential company interested in buying you, remember that due diligence is just as important when selling your company as it was when you first set it up.

Important Reminders Are Worth Repeating

Highlight Tangible Assets: It's a sad fact that many banks are still hesitant to lend money for the purchase of businesses. You could, of course, offer seller financing, but another way to go is to highlight your tangible assets. Buyers of businesses with considerable tangible assets such as real estate or capital equipment are having more luck securing bank loans. By providing a comprehensive list of your tangible assets, the prospect of securing bank financing becomes more real when the acquisition includes tangible assets, which carry their own value.

Do Your Own Due Diligence: Before you agree to sell anything, do your own due diligence on your own company before anyone from the outside does. Hire a friendly accountant to come in and look at the books. If he identifies any skeletons in the closet, you will be better prepared to deal with them before the buyer ever finds out. Once the buyer spots it, he can and likely will use it as a way to chip away at the price.

Weed out Speculators: Once you have completed the cursory discussions and have executed all appropriate agreements, ask for a non-refundable deposit before beginning negotiations. This tactic will weed out anyone who isn't serious about potentially buying your business. At the very minimum, consider arming your Confidentiality Agreement with a sizable financial penalty should the wannabe buyer gets loose lips.

Keep It Confidential: I've said it before, but it's worth saying again. Avoid advertising the fact that you want to sell your business; it could be taken as a sign the business is in distress. You don't want your competitors, suppliers, customers, or employees gossiping about the "problems" in your business. Approach targeted buyers under the pretense of looking for teaming arrangements or other working partnerships to first ascertain their level of interest. Remember the Confidentiality Agreement with a penalty provision.

Recognize That You May Need to Stay On: As we have discussed previously, many former owners find it difficult to stay on after they have sold the business. Despite these obvious challenges, the buyer may well make it a condition of sale. At the very least, they will probably make you sign a Non-Compete Agreement. If so, be sure you are happy not being able to compete for a reasonable period of time or having to stay on to oversee succession. Give this issue serious thought, both in terms of possibly staying on or not being able to compete against your former company. Inasmuch as you might say neither is an issue for you, there will come a time when you wished you had not agreed to do either.

Don't Give Unlimited Warranties: Avoid unlimited warranties or personal guarantees at all costs. You may find that you cannot keep them or that trying to do so places an unreasonable restriction on you.

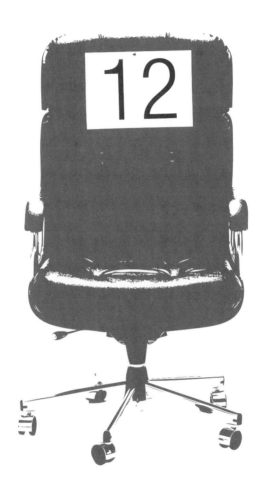

An Absentee Owner: Staying in the Game

There is always the plausible chance you cannot sell your company, or you cannot sell it the way you want. In these instances you have a decision to make; do you simply hold onto the company and work it until you can find a buyer, or do you let someone else operate it while you play the role of absentee owner?

The scenario of the absentee owner comes in two forms. The first relates to the idea of staying on after the new owner has taken control, while the second scenario centers on an inability to find a buyer and allowing your management team to operate the company on your behalf.

While the first scenario has been discussed on numerous occasions throughout this book, the latter may be an appealing alternative. If the reason you're selling is primarily because you've just had enough—burnout is a common reason for small businesses to go on the market—could being an absentee owner solve all of your problems? Could you hire someone to manage the business and then take a step back?

It's not the same as a sale, and it has some concerns, but it's something we should consider. The key to getting what you want from you company to fund your retirement is to examine all of your options, so let's assess the idea of being an absentee owner.

Could You Be an Absentee Owner?

Absentee ownership is certainly not for everyone. Back when you started your company, you were anything and everything but an absentee owner. When your business began to grow, and it needed constant attention to detail, you were not an absentee owner. Following your growth phase, the business began to mature, and you needed a stronger and deeper management team to help move it forward. You did not play the role of an absentee owner.

What are the character traits of an effective absentee owner? Before we can consider the answer to this important question, perhaps we need to assess the company first. The optimum question is whether your company is prepared for an absentee owner. In many ways, businesses need babysitting. We all know that if you do not pay attention to the details, even for a mature company, strategic initiatives get watered down, costs tend to rise, and the staff gets too comfortable in thinking all they have to do is show up, do what is customary, and profits roll in.

Your company, like a vast majority owned by aging Baby Boomers, is probably too small to allow you to take your eyes completely off the road that lies ahead. Like most, your company needs guidance and the occasional swift kick-in-the-pants. As the owner, you have learned to keep your foot on the gas pedal, otherwise profits inevitably suffer. Even the best management teams get lackadaisical at times because they have come to rely on your vision, energy, and perseverance.

You have become their safety net. So, again, before you can even consider becoming an absentee owner, you really need to assess your company's ability to operate itself. Yes, you will still have first line supervisors, managers, and directors. The company will continue to adhere to its operating procedures and policy guidance, and its customers will buy your products and/or services. But despite the obviousness that business will continue in some capacity, will it continue to generate the profits you want and need to supplement your retirement if you are not sitting in the big chair?

As an absentee owner, you can pop in when you like, but you're not committed to be in the office or factory every single hour of every single day like you used to be. Instead, you're watching from afar, ready to swoop in should you be needed. Oh, and you're getting your regular paycheck as well.

For those of you who do not have an exit strategy in mind, this option sounds like the perfect solution, doesn't it? But could it really work for you and your company?

Well, let me just say now that it might not be quite the rosy picture that you're imagining. You see, being an absentee owner can actually be a lot harder—and much more frustrating—than it looks.

The first question, of course, is who would be your day-to-day manager? Do you have someone in the company who could do it now, or will you need to recruit from outside? If you have to do the latter, there's going to be a period of transition where you need to show the new boss the ropes. If you have an internal manager successor, the same still applies.

A new outside manager will not know your company as well as the internal candidates. The managers you now have in place will likely resent the new manager, so how you select, transition, and educate both the new manager and your staff is critically important.

Then there's the inside option. Imagine you have a few managers in your company who would all be interested in the position; what do you do?

You could appoint a management team to handle the day-to-day running of the company for you, BUT will they all play nice together? Will they be vying for control and fighting each other instead of pushing the company forward? Likewise, if any one of them is a powerful personality, there are probably going to be ramifications as the others resent his/her overwhelming exercise of authority.

This is where you need to make what may be an unpopular choice no matter which way you decide to go. This is where the question of character traits comes into play. What are the character traits of an absentee owner? First and foremost, without any question or hesitation, the most critically important trait needed for an absentee owner is the ability to delegate.

Delegation is often misunderstood, especially by business owners. Yes, you have delegated tasks all your professional life. You have some staffers doing this and some doing that. By your best recollection, most delegated tasks have turned out okay. Where they haven't, you certainly didn't make the same mistake twice — or so most business owners think. In essence, you are thinking in terms of the "art of delegation."

The art of delegation centers on the simple process of getting the right people in the room, telling them what you need and expect from them, giving them some metrics and due dates, and letting them loose. In this simple context, you are correct; you have delegated tasks to your staffers and they understand what you want and when. It sounds easy and straightforward because it is. The "art" aspect of delegation is much like a painting; beauty (and in this case, effectiveness) is in the eye of the beholder. Because you think the delegation was done effectively, you also expect the results to be achieved. In many cases, this is nothing but wishful thinking.

The effectiveness of delegation lies not in the "art" of its application but rather in the "science" of how it is carried out. The "science of delegation" centers on the follow-up: were the necessary and required results achieved, and if not, why and what does it mean to the company going forward? This is where most business owners fall short. In too many cases, when a delegated task is not achieved, the business owner likely says and does the wrong thing; they tend to do it themselves the next time. Not only is this the wrong thing to do if you want your business to become more efficient and profitable, this response keeps you at the center of attention. When it comes to considering whether you are a viable candidate to be an absentee owner, you will fail.

Absentee owners, above anything and everything else, must be effective in the "science of delegation." If you can't, or won't, hold your managers' feet to the fire and make them accountable, you should not consider being an absentee owner. The risks are simply too great as your life's work and wealth is tied to your individual ability should you choose this option. At the end of the day, you can't hide behind anyone else, and if you cannot delegate effectively, the only ones to be hurt in the end is you, your family, and your wallet.

Your Role

There are a lot of other things that you're going to need to think about if you want to go down the route of being an absentee owner. The most obvious is deciding what your personal role will be in the company now that you're not there all the time.

What decisions will you make, and what will you delegate to the manager? How much time should, or would, you want to spend on the business? How can you do so and still keep up with the competition? And the crucial question—how do you monitor your business as an absentee owner?

All of these things, of course, may well depend on what you want to do with your time away from the business during your retirement; if you want to travel, for instance, that's certainly going to limit the time you can physically be on hand if the company runs into problems.

Likewise, if you've always dreamed of retiring to Palm Springs, but your company is in Maine, that's a fair distance. Are you prepared to spend a significant portion of your retirement traveling to and from? Alternatively, are you happy to be so far away and so distant from the company?

It may well be, therefore, that your retirement plans just aren't compatible with being an absentee owner, so before you think of going down this road, spend a little time working out exactly what it is you do want to do in your later years. Don't just think of your life now, of course; think of it in another ten or 20 years.

You may be easily mobile now, but what happens in five or ten years? What about the health of your spouse or significant other? Just how happy will you be to get on a plane to see your company then?

It's tempting to think that you will adjust; you may even think that keeping your company but having the freedom to own or manage it absently is worth giving up some of those dreams you had for retirement. But don't be presumptuous. Your retirement is forever; it's what you've been working towards all this time.

Your company was your gateway to retirement, remember? It was your passport to freedom, your opportunity to do all the things you wanted to do later in life. Are you now saying that your company is actually a shackle instead? This is exactly the kind of thinking this book is trying to get you to lose. *The Exit Equation* is predicated on coming to terms with what is important to you and to do so as objectively as possible. From this position, and only from this position, can you derive the best strategy to achieve your dreams and ambitions. Too many times over the years you have compromised, and so has your family. Whenever your company needed you; you were there. If it needed cash; you infused what was required. Your vacations centered around your work schedule and peak seasons. And now, here you are yet again, thinking about compromising what is important to you.

My advice to you would be not to sacrifice *anything*; if being an absentee owner is the right thing to do for you, you should be able to do it without surrendering your dreams.

That's a key part of this decision, of course. It may sound contrary, but would being an absentee owner actually trap you more than it frees you? If you don't have the liquidity to do as you want (because you never actually sold your company), that could well be the case.

Even if you sold part of your company but want to stay on as an absentee owner after the sale, would the relationship be practical and functional?

Transitioning Into an Absentee Owner

The idea of being free to choose when you go into work (or not) is appealing, but as soon as most people really begin to think about being an absentee owner, there's one fear that seems to just grow and grow: will I lose control of my business?

Most small business owners are control freaks; we've had to be to make sure everything gets done, on time and in the way we want it. That control-freakery was part of our job description. So can you really give it up now?

What happens if your employees don't run the company the way you want them to when you are not there? What if customers stop buying from you? What if, God forbid, there are problems with the company that you won't even know about because you're not there or your management keeps them from you?

Monitoring Your Company

Everything mentioned thus far as it relates to being an absentee owner is pertinent. These things can, and often do, happen. In reality, your employees shouldn't be able to run the business into the ground if you have set up systems and procedures they must follow AND if you monitor your company's performance on a regular basis.

Don't fool yourself into thinking that you can monitor company performance whenever you have the time. That's just not going to work. If you truly want an absentee ownership to work, you can't be quite as absent as you may think.

You see, here's the rub. Being an absentee owner is actually a proactive process. It's not necessarily an easy option. If you want your company to continue succeeding, you can't just take off and forget about your business. You need to spend a fair amount of time looking through the financial metrics and reports needed to assess the continued performance of your company. In addition to the standard operating issues, make sure you do not leave strategic planning to the whims and wishes of your manager or management team. You have always been the strategist, and until your team shows signs of fulfilling this important task, make sure you take the time each year to chart a course for success—just like you did when you were there. Remember what the prize is—your money and getting it out of your business on your terms.

Letting Go of the Control Freak Within You

There's another danger to this monitoring thing and that is how do you walk that fine line between monitoring and interfering for the sake of your wallet? In an ideal world, you will check your operating metrics, financials, and management reports and decide you're happy with it—or if you're not, you'll have a conversation with your manager—and then, assuming there is no big crisis, move on.

But can you do that? Can you really give up the control freak tendencies within you, the ones that every good business owner has and has relied on heavily in the past?

There will be lots of differences in perspective when you're an absentee owner; maybe a manager has offered concessions to a sale that you never would have made, for instance. Perhaps another has ignored one of the perfectly good systems you put in place and has done things his own way. Maybe a unmotivated employee is taking more sick days than is permitted, or you have a customer complaint that does not get addressed by your manager with the same conviction you would have exemplified. Are you going to deal with these issues yourself? If so, you will undermine all you have set out to do and will likely find yourself right back in the same chair doing the same things you have done for years.

Be honest with yourself: if you know you're likely to get sucked into the day-to-day running of the business, being an absentee owner is not for you.

Keeping Relationships

One potentially big danger associated with being an absentee owner is that you lose the relationships you had with customers, vendors, officials, and even your employees. Personal relationships are especially important to small businesses; they are the lifeblood of what you do and how successfully you are doing it. In the end, business is based and built on loyalty; without relationships your business will certainly suffer.

Leaving the company to become an absentee owner can mean that you lose customers. There's no getting away from the fact that some customers will miss you and may leave the relationship you have maintained with them over the years simply because they would rather deal with you than with someone else. I enjoyed a long-term business relationship with one of my clients. As his travels and employment exploits moved him around the country, he always made it a point to use the services of my consulting company. Over the years we had created an understanding of how the projects needed to work, I knew what he needed to justify a project and how the results were to be explained, he could trust the details of my work and the confidentiality of the data, and we collectively completed projects faster and more efficiently than anyone else. He prospered as did my company. Our working relationship was so strong I never asked him to sign a contract, and he never asked me to adjust my price.

Eventually I sold my company and, as a result, he stopped using my former firm. It wasn't about the expertise that remained behind, and it wasn't about any lack of service. It was about trust and confidence. My situation is no different than most business owners who have built their businesses on relationships. People do business with people they trust, and if you become an absentee owner, there may be some customers/clients who are ill at ease with what's left for them to use if you are not there.

Employees too may miss you and may even resent the fact that you are no longer around; their loyalty may even waiver to a degree. Never underestimate how much pride employees take in impressing the boss; it's a great motivational tool. If the boss is never there, however, and shows no interest in the well-being of the company and its staff, why should an employee go the extra mile?

This is where you again need to make your presence felt; pop in to the company regularly and have meetings with employees to show you are still in control. Work hard to engender a feeling of motivation even if you don't happen to be in the office all the time. In short, don't be quite as absent as the title "absentee owner" suggests.

All of which is again short code for "you must be proactively involved in your company," even if you are an absentee owner. Your company is your investment; you must show up consistently and keep on top of it just as you would if you had invested in the stock market.

If you're reading this chapter and getting the idea that I'm not a fan of the absentee owner, I'll be honest with you: you're right! I have seen few absentee owner companies that actually work; there always seem to be so many issues thrown up just by virtue of the fact that the owner isn't there that it seems both counter-intuitive and counter-productive.

I've also seen absentee owners who loved the idea of being free to enjoy their retirement while still having a company behind them and a regular paycheck but who end up absolutely *hating* their decision.

But they especially struggle with the idea that someone else is making the decisions for them. It's your company; *you* should be the one in control. Even those absentee owners with a great manager or management team and constant communication often end up resenting the fact that someone else is now in the big chair and their livelihood is in someone else's hands.

Of those absentee owners who have made it work (sort of), they have one thing in common. They're not really quite as absent as they planned to be. They got sucked back into the day-to-day, some of them even going so far as to go back full-time.

Others swoop into the company once a month or more frequently, spending days meeting everyone, getting their presence re-established, spending their time recalibrating the team…and they resent every single minute of it. It's an unusual small business owner who is happy with other people knowing more about their company than they do.

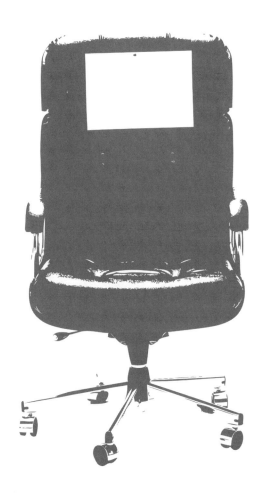

The Underlying Principles
of *The Exit Equation...*

When it comes to selling your business, don't underestimate just how emotional and potentially traumatic the whole process can be. I don't say this to dissuade you, but to prepare you. It may well be the most emotionally confusing experience you will ever have, and you may well be the most conflicted you have ever been.

These feelings are the result of selling your pride and joy—the business you nursed to life from scratch. You were there the day your company became part of you. Now here you are, some years later, considering how to best let it go. It's no wonder that you may have doubts about your decision and questions as to whether you are going about it the right way.

Every business owner finds themselves in a unique situation. Inasmuch as you have a lot in common with other business owners, the reality is that each of you has specific issues, considerations, and expectations. It can be said no two business owners are the same, but there is not much difference between them.

So now, here you are considering the unthinkable. What was once merely a thought on the horizon is now facing you dead-on. Do you sell, and if so, how? Do you stay, and if so, why? It's no wonder you're emotionally conflicted, but now is the time to come to grips with what you want and need to do in your life.

Selling your business can be a tough proposition, especially in this market. I hope that I have given you the insight and information you need to make it happen. This book is crammed full of tips, hints, and solutions to even the most complicated scenarios.

If there's just one thing that I would want you to take from this book, it would be this: think of yourself. That's THE most important thing to remember in all your exit planning and sale negotiations:

PUT YOURSELF FIRST.

It's not something we're encouraged to do often, is it? We grow up constantly being told to think of others, and we live our adult life repeatedly being told not to be too greedy. This perspective is magnified when we consider the needs and wants of our business and the responsibilities that come with the package. But despite what you are used to, change is inevitable. As Brad Pitt stated in his role as Billy Beane in the movie, Moneyball, "adapt or die".

There are plenty of books on the market that tout the five secrets of selling your business, or the seven tips to get out rich, or the nine options to consider when it's time to retire. What no one ever talks about is you, the owner: why you should get out, when to do it, what to consider, how you need to leverage your knowledge, and who you need to use. The Exit Equation is based on the fundamental concept that in order to get out with your money and on your terms, you need to start with the end in mind; and that end is you. What you need and what you want to do is the basis of an effective exit strategy.

You're not being greedy by putting yourself first. It is a necessity because your business will not prosper if you remain at the helm but do not have the drive or passion to make it work. Your employees know when you are on your game, and they know when you are not. If you realize it's time to go, so do your employees. You can serve the interests of all, just like you have done time and time again during your ownership, by putting yourself first and then developing a succession plan that expounds on the greatest attributes of your company to push you and it to greater achievements.

You set up a business that you intended to look after you in your retirement; you sacrificed and scrimped, missed your children's music recitals and football games, probably earned a few choice words from your spouse along the way, and no doubt would have loved to have spent a lot more of your time either at home or out with friends, but you didn't…you spent it working on your business instead. All so you could look after yourself and your family in retirement.

That's why I have absolutely no qualms in telling you to put yourself first and the rest will come more clearly into focus. It is from this perspective that the exit strategy you never gave heed to will begin to formulate, and you will achieve what you never dreamt would come your way.

Now some of you will question the notion of identifying what you want to do in retirement. Your argument will be there is no way of telling what the future will bring and what its requirements will be. Although true to a degree, don't hide behind the shallow fears because in the end, your life's work has been done, and now your life's enjoyment needs to commence.

Work out what you want or need to get from the sale in order to finance the next, best phase of your life, and go for it. Ignore all the other competing demands and make sure you secure the things that really matter to you. As I've said in almost every single chapter throughout this book, you can't really look after yourself effectively without knowing what you want to do with the next phase of your life; that's the second most important lesson to learn from this book. An effective plan starts with your plan for the future. Once you accept that fact, your interests must be served first; the next step is to determine what it is you want to do. These decisions will lead to the formation of a plan that considers time, expectations, and capacity of your company. If the company can meet your needs, then a sale is close at hand. If your company is ill-prepared to generate what you need from a sale, then you will need to fix what ails it before you can proceed.

Knowing what you want to do in your retirement can dictate everything from the price you ask for the company, to who you potentially sell it to and what sacrificial lambs you have in mind during the sales process, as well as the terms and conditions you will accept for the sale and when you will put the company on the market in the first place.

Let's briefly re-cap the advice offered in this book:

Don't Leave It Too Late

If you stay with your company until the day you wake up and decide "enough is enough," you're doing yourself and your business a disservice. You shouldn't sell your company when you don't really want to and certainly not before you need to. Sell when your company is on the rise. Remember, a buyer almost always wants to be able to put their mark on the acquisition, and they often will buy a company that is not running on all eight cylinders. Trust me; in most cases your exit plan will take three to five years of planning and hard work before it is ready for sale.

Don't Miss the Point

Your company wasn't meant to be the be all and end all; it must serve a purpose for you when it is time for you to retire and move on. In short, it was intended to be your retirement plan. Don't get bogged down with the day-to-day, and don't get emotional; treat your business as the passport to what's next in your life. Don't let it stand in your way.

Make Your Own Future

Come to grips with what is important to you in the next phase of your life. By creating your own plans and your own buy-out scenarios, you can take control of your sale and better understand what a potential buyer will want and how you can frame your company to deliver it.

Systems, Systems, Systems

Systems work when you don't. Buyers, especially sophisticated buyers, want to see how the company runs. Systems help to achieve this outcome and deliver the results a buyer is looking for. The other important consideration is that as you work on your company during the time horizon needed to prepare it for sale, systems can help assure you things are being done the right way. Systems help buyers and sellers alike, and they are the key to sustained profitability.

It's All Important but…It's Really Just the Frosting on the Cake

Never forget the key point in a sale negotiation: a buyer is looking for something, and your job is to find out what it is as early in the process as you can. Everything else is just frosting on the cake. If you can't determine the key drivers to the sale, your sale will never get off the ground.

Think Terms, Not Just Price

Terms dictate price. Don't get fixated on price because it is an unnecessary hurdle that stymies most sales. If you have been honest with yourself as to what is important to you in your post-ownership days, you will come to the conclusion the terms of your sale trump the price every time.

Don't Confuse Price With Value

Price and value are NOT the same; the price of your business is what someone will pay for it. The value is what the company is actually worth. Many business owners over-value their businesses because they simply do not objectively assess the bankability of the transaction. Remember, if you have been taking an above market salary, enjoying lavish corporate business "trips," have passed a variety of your living expenses onto the company, drive an expensive corporate car filled with corporate gas, and have access to a liberal expense report, you have been enjoying your sales price early. Each dollar you take out of your company has a direct impact on the sales price. You can't have it both ways!

Willing Buyers and Sellers…Meeting in the Middle

Consensus, not compromise. This is the mantra of every

consummated business transaction. You can put your own price on the company, but there's one thing you need to understand: your company is only worth what someone will pay for it. Willing buyers and willing sellers are what make the world—or the business sales world—go round. The biggest reason that small businesses don't sell is because the buyer and seller have very different ideas of what they're willing to pay or accept. As stated earlier in this re-cap, listen, listen, listen. If you want to make the sale work, and you want it to work to your advantage, listen to what the buyer is saying.

The Misconception About Money

There's no doubt that cold hard cash brings you the freedom to chase your dreams and to live your retirement the way you want, but that doesn't mean that money is all you want. There will be certain things you want from your sale that can't be measured in dollars—give them the respect they deserve!

Choosing a Successor

If it makes sense for your business to transition to an internal buyer, don't let emotion, loyalty or duty sway your choice. Be dispassionate about a potential successor of your business and do the same things required of an external sale. Consider the options carefully because internal sales come with significant baggage. Choose the right person, for the right reason. Make sure they are bankable, risk-tolerable and cut out for the job.

Pulling the Trigger

Business owners are their own worst enemies. For all they are good at, and for the many things accomplished over the years, crafting a successful exit strategy is a mountain many business owners doubt they can conquer.

All too often, I find that business owners are poor strategic planners and horrible managers. Yes, they have had a steady, driving hand in all the company has achieved. Their ability to meet each challenge and morph themselves and their companies into a better and stronger entity is uncanny. But this ability has been developed over time and often through testing, failure, and retesting. Day-to-day business tends to support this type of learning curve, especially once the company begins to generate sustained, positive cash flow. But an exit strategy is different. The learning curve is steep and somewhat unforgiving. It is imperative to do it right the first time because each succeeding opportunity tends to water down the return on investment.

Consider the Story of Bob

Bob is a business owner who started his construction company with a borrowed backhoe and an old, dilapidated dump truck. He had worked in the industry for a few years, was high school educated, and felt he could do it differently. He worked damn hard when he started, putting in many hours on the job and away from his young family to make sure he made ends meet. It wasn't about success inasmuch as it was about survival. He had never been in business before, didn't go to school for it, probably had never heard the word entrepreneur let alone knew how to spell it, and made his share of mistakes. But he learned, adapted, and took risks that, back then, didn't seem as risky as they were necessary.

Over the ensuing years, Bob got better at being a business owner. His procedures were more the result of common sense and purpose than they were about profits and growth. He hired based on his gut, and he kicked guys in the ass who needed it. The good ones simply continued to get their paychecks each week, and that was fine with them. Bob was loyal, and his crew followed suit. Certainly some left for perceived greener pastures, but the ones that stayed became family. They worked, drank, and recreated together. The business began to gain some traction. Bob learned about finance and credit. He made sure he made his payments, and he began to understand the importance of operational efficiency even though he didn't know what it meant.

Bob started to make some money—real money. His decisions became riskier. He leveraged what he knew and what he owned to get the next big job. His staff grew, as did his payroll. He started to have ulcers. Banks began to court him. He felt bigger than life and began to live it that way. Eventually he hired an accountant to help him manage his financial affairs, and he hired an attorney because the projects he pursued were often won in court, the result of changing conditions and acts of God. The construction industry is a dog-eat-dog world, and Bob became a player. Eventually Bob listened to his accountant and began to diversify his growing wealth. He bought property. He bought a bigger house. New cars were gifts to himself and rewards for a job well done. Bob didn't forget about his employees. Better fringe benefits, company trucks to his lieutenants, bonuses for all, and lavish parties were the benefits of hard work and long hours. Money was flowing, and life was good.

As the business continued to flourish, Bob worked hard but tended to play harder. His personal expenditures on the company trough grew larger. He diversified into a land developer, a formula that leveraged the attributes of his business with the opportunity in the marketplace. The risks were more pronounced, but the paydays were enormous. Bob's ulcer got bigger, and his health suffered. He took more time away from his company, leaving the daily operations to his key managers. Bob was as much leveraged at the bank as he was in his company and life.

After some 30 years at the helm, Bob wants to get out. He's older and feels it. The recent economic downturn has put a chink in his armor. The accountant is spending more time strategizing the dismantling of the company and its assets than he used to provide to Bob to help build the company. Projects are harder to come by because competition has gotten stiffer. It could be said Bob fell asleep at the wheel. His successes spoiled him even though he would never admit it. The company, by the very nature of its characteristics and demands, won't let Bob go. You see, large construction projects require bonding, and since Bob is the sole shareholder, the ability of his company to compete and retain future projects rests solely with the largeness and earning capacity of Bob's wallet. Bob's exit options are limited. Bob is not a planner. This is a bad mix.

Bob is finally considering the next phase of his life. He is tired, and his health is not what it once was. His fortune has shrunk as a result of the economy and his own inability to "adapt or die." You see, bigger was always better for Bob. He grew because the profits were worth the risks. Yes, he was provided financial guidance and legal support. But what Bob didn't have was a plan, an exit plan. He simply did what he has always done and never really considered how to get out, let alone when. His lieutenants are not successor material. They have lived under the shadow of the man for many years and do not possess his appetite for risk but prefer the comfort of his wallet.

What can Bob do? How do you go about making amends for not starting out with the end in mind? Bob is the prototypical baby boomer-aged business owner. My suggestion is for Bob to begin the exit planning process by deciding what is important to him now rather than living with the dreams of the past. How much money is enough, and how much time is needed for him to do the things he now deems important? If Bob is not careful, he will begin to live life under the shadow of his greatest regret.

Epilogue

It is my sincere hope this book provides the insight, perspective, and knowledge you need to live your life out of the shadow of your business. What was once important probably isn't as important anymore. Times change, as do people and business owners. I realize you are probably really good at what you do, and your business has given you many of the things you enjoy. In many ways, you will rationalize the cash your company gives you. You will argue it is too much to give up, especially for a dream that remains unclear. As stated in the Prologue of this book, wealth does not come from starting a company, and it does not come from operating and growing a company. True wealth comes from selling a company.

You can make a great sale if you start with the end in mind and begin the process of introspection. The Exit Equation begins and ends with you. Your company has the ability to suck you into the black hole and never let you go if you don't put yourself first. Your money and your terms can become a reality if you develop a plan and stick to it. If you are a good businessperson, you can do it. Excuses have never held you back before.

I wish you all the very best in your efforts to achieve escape velocity. Life is better after you leave.